Theme Skills Tests
Table of Contents

Practice Test 1

Theme 1: Courage 3
  A. Noting Details 4
  B. Making Judgments .6
  C. Sequence of Events 8
  D. Predicting Outcomes 10
  E. Information and Study Skills 12
  F. Suffixes *-ful, -less,* and *-ly* 14
  G. Syllabication 15
  H. Prefixes *un-* and *re-* 16
  I. Possessives and Contractions 17
  J. Spelling 18
  K. Vocabulary 20
  L. Grammar 22
  M. Writing Skills 25

Theme 2: What Really Happened? 27
  A. Fact and Opinion 28
  B. Making Inferences 30
  C. Text Organization 32
  D. Information and Study Skills 34
  E. "Someone Who" Suffixes 36
  F. Inflected Endings *-s, -es* 37
  G. Adjective Suffixes *-al, -ive, -ous* 38
  H. Spelling 39
  I. Vocabulary 41
  J. Grammar 43
  K. Writing Skills 45

Theme 3: Growing Up .47
  A. Making Generalizations 48
  B. Making Inferences 50
  C. Story Structure 52
  D. Problem Solving and Decision Making 54
  E. Information and Study Skills 56
  F. VCV, VCCV, and VCCCV Patterns 58
  G. Words Ending in *-ed* or *-ing* 59
  H. Endings and Suffixes *-en, -ize, -ify* 60
  I. Prefixes *in-, im-,* and *con-* 61

J   Spelling 62
K. Vocabulary 64
L. Grammar 67
M. Writing Skills 69

Theme 4: Discovering Ancient Cultures 71
A. Author's Viewpoint: Bias and Assumption 72
B. Cause and Effect 74
C. Topic, Main Idea, and Details 76
D. Information and Study Skills 78
E. Suffixes -ic, -al, and -ure 80
F. Suffixes -ion and -ation 81
G. Unstressed Syllables 82
H. Spelling 83
I. Vocabulary 85
J. Grammar 87
K. Writing Skills 89

Theme 5: Doers and Dreamers 91
A. Propaganda 92
B. Problem Solving 94
C. Compare and Contrast 96
D. Information and Study Skills 98
E. Word Parts ven and graph 100
F. Plurals 101
G. Suffixes -ent/-ence, -ant/-ance, -able/-ible, -ate 102
H. Spelling 103
I. Vocabulary 105
J. Grammar 107
K. Writing Skills 109

Theme 6: New Frontiers: Oceans and Space 111
A. Cause and Effect 112
B. Following Directions 114
C. Categorize and Classify 116
D. Drawing Conclusions 118
E. Information and Study Skills 120
F. Prefixes de-, dis-, ex-, inter-, per-, pre-, pro- 122
G. Prefixes ad- and ob- 123
H. Words with ie or ei 124
I. Word Parts 125
J. Spelling 126
K. Vocabulary 128
L. Grammar 130
M. Writing Skills 132

Name _____

Practice Test

Read the passage and answer the question that follows. Fill in the circle next to the best answer.

A campfire can help you survive in the wilderness. It provides warmth and helps your body conserve heat. It also keeps insects and wild animals away. A campfire dries wet clothing and boots. A warm meal cooked over a campfire gives you energy and tastes great! In an emergency, a campfire can mean the difference between life and death — it can be used to signal for help.

1. What is the passage describing?
- ○ **A.** how to build a campfire
- ○ **B.** where to build a campfire
- ○ **C.** the importance of a campfire
- ○ **D.** how to start a campfire

Courage

Level 6, Theme 1

Theme Skills Test Record

Student _____ Date _____

Student Record Form

	Possible Score	Criterion Score	Student Score
Part A: Noting Details	5	4	
Part B: Making Judgments	5	4	
Part C: Sequence of Events	5	4	
Part D: Predicting Outcomes	5	4	
Part E: Information and Study Skills	5	4	
Part F: Suffixes *-ful, -less,* and *-ly*	5	4	
Part G: Syllabication	5	4	
Part H: Prefixes *un-* and *re-*	5	4	
Part I: Possessives and Contractions	5	4	
Part J: Spelling	10	8	
Part K: Vocabulary	10	8	
Part L: Grammar	10	8	
Part M: Writing Skills	5	4	
TOTAL	80	64	
Total Student Score x 1.25 =			%

Name _____

Noting Details

Read the passage and answer the questions that follow. Fill in the circle next to the best answer.

The Storm

Lightning flashed in the distance, followed by low, rumbling thunder. Marta glanced out the window. She remembered other spring storms that had turned violent. Back then, her mom had hurried Marta and her little sister Amy into the storm cellar. Now, though, Mom was at work. Marta, who was thirteen, watched Amy when they both got home from school.

Marta switched on the television. A typed message crawled along the bottom of the screen. A tornado watch had been issued. Worried, Marta pushed open the screen door and called to Amy, "You'd better come in now."

The girls had just begun their homework when the phone rang. "Marta, they have spotted a tornado heading in your direction," Mom said in a strained voice. "Get to the cellar, quickly. Get word to Mrs. Garza if you —." Just then, a bolt of lightning cracked through the sky, and the phone line went dead.

Grabbing Amy's hand, Marta headed toward the storm cellar in the backyard. She pulled back the heavy cellar door and helped Amy down the stairs. Then she remembered Mrs. Garza.

"Stay put," Marta yelled to Amy as she closed the cellar door. Marta dashed across the yard and through the fence gate. She did not knock but ran right into Mrs. Garza's kitchen. The gray-haired woman looked up in surprise. "Come with me, quickly," said Marta. She helped Mrs. Garza to her feet and led her through the pouring rain to the storm cellar. As she pulled the door shut, Marta heard a roaring noise above her. The heavy door shook wildly. Marta, Amy, and Mrs. Garza huddled together near the back of the cellar.

As quickly as it began, the storm was over. Marta raised the cellar door and peered out. Tree limbs, roof pieces, and broken glass were scattered everywhere. Marta's quick action had kept them all from harm.

1. Which detail from the first paragraph lets you know the story is set in spring?

   ○ **A.** There was thunder and lightning.
   ○ **B.** Marta and Amy were still in school.
   ○ **C.** Marta's family had a storm cellar.
   ○ **D.** Marta remembered other spring storms.

2. How do you know that this story takes place in modern times?

   ○ **F.** Marta switched on a television.
   ○ **G.** Marta pushed open a screen door.
   ○ **H.** Amy was playing outside.
   ○ **J.** Marta's mom was not at home.

3. Why is Mom's voice strained on the telephone?

   ○ **A.** She was proud because the girls were doing their homework.
   ○ **B.** She was angry because Marta and Amy had been watching television.
   ○ **C.** She was worried because she had heard a tornado was headed toward the girls.
   ○ **D.** She was tired because she had been at work all day.

4. Which detail helps you know that Mrs. Garza is Marta's next-door neighbor?

   ○ **F.** Marta dashed through her fence gate to get to Mrs. Garza's house.
   ○ **G.** Marta's mom told her to get in touch with Mrs. Garza.
   ○ **H.** Marta did not knock when she got to Mrs. Garza's house.
   ○ **J.** Marta found Mrs. Garza in the kitchen and helped her to her feet.

5. Which detail does **not** help you know that there was a dangerously strong wind in the storm?

   ○ **A.** Marta heard a roaring noise above her as she closed the cellar door.
   ○ **B.** Marta, Amy, and Mrs. Garza all huddled together near the back of the cellar.
   ○ **C.** The heavy cellar door shook wildly after Marta closed it.
   ○ **D.** Tree limbs, roof pieces, and broken glass were scattered everywhere.

STOP

Name _____

Making Judgments

Read the passage and answer the questions that follow. Fill in the circle next to the best answer.

The Stolen Purse

Long ago, a farmer named Silas was walking toward his stall in the outdoor market. Silas worked hard on his farm, but there was little produce left to sell after he fed his family. Today he had only five apples and four cabbages in his pack. He hoped to earn enough to buy spring vegetable seeds.

As Silas reached his stall, he noticed something lying on the path. He reached down and picked up a small leather purse. Inside, Silas discovered 100 gold coins. It was more money than he had ever seen or even imagined! Just then, Silas heard a man's voice yelling, "I'll pay a reward to anyone who finds my purse!"

Closing the purse, Silas held it up and called to the man, who rushed over. He grabbed the purse from Silas, opened it, then turned to walk away.

"But I have returned your purse. What about the reward?" asked Silas.

"Reward!" the man shouted. "I should have you arrested for stealing my money. There were 200 coins in this purse and now there are only 100. Leave me alone or I will call for help."

About that time, a judge who had overheard the exchange walked up. He knew something of both men and was disturbed by what was happening.

"Why don't you allow me to settle this matter," said the judge. The two men, knowing the judge's position of importance, quickly agreed and handed him the purse.

"I believe that both of you are telling the truth," said the judge. "Silas says the purse he found contains 100 gold coins. You," he said, speaking to the other man, "lost a purse containing 200 pieces of gold. The purse Silas found couldn't possibly be yours." Then the judge gave the purse and the 100 gold coins back to Silas.

This story has a moral: If you have the courage to do what is right, your actions may be richly rewarded.

1. Based on information in the first paragraph, what can you tell about Silas?
   ○ **A.** He is willing to work hard for little reward.
   ○ **B.** He is a good salesman but a poor farmer.
   ○ **C.** He spends his hard-earned money foolishly.
   ○ **D.** His family is not very important to him.

2. How do you know that Silas is an honest man?
   ○ **F.** He has a stall in the market.
   ○ **G.** He picks up the leather purse.
   ○ **H.** He returns the purse to its owner.
   ○ **J.** He asks for the promised reward.

3. Which is the best description of the man who lost the purse?
   ○ **A.** He is wealthy and enjoys fine things.
   ○ **B.** He only respects people he knows well.
   ○ **C.** He is smart enough to earn a lot of money.
   ○ **D.** He is greedy and disrespectful.

4. Silas asked the man to give him the reward. What does this help you know about Silas?
   ○ **F.** He is not afraid to ask for what he thinks he deserves.
   ○ **G.** He is just as greedy as the man who lost the purse.
   ○ **H.** He wants to buy some things for his family.
   ○ **J.** He does not want to have to work for his money.

5. What kind of person is the judge?
   ○ **A.** He is an important man, and he wants everyone to know it.
   ○ **B.** He is kind only to people who work hard for a living.
   ○ **C.** He is a friendly man who enjoys visiting with the people of the village.
   ○ **D.** He is a wise man who knows how to deal fairly with people.

Name _____

Sequence of Events

Read the passage and answer the questions that follow. Fill in the circle next to the best answer.

Trouble at Sea

Keesha, her brother Shaun, and their Uncle Ted sailed out of Long Beach, California, early on a foggy morning. They stopped for a while on Catalina Island. Then the three set sail for San Diego. A gentle breeze filled the sails on the *Sea Gull*. Keesha thought her uncle had given his sailboat the perfect name. When the wind was right, the pretty boat seemed to fly over the water. It was a beautiful day, and everything was going great until the mainsail became caught in the rigging.

"Don't worry," said Uncle Ted. "I'll have this fixed in no time." He easily climbed up toward the snag. Then, without warning, a gust of wind rocked the boat. Uncle Ted gave a sharp cry as he slipped and fell to the deck. "My leg," he moaned. "I think I've broken my leg."

Keesha and Shaun rushed to help their uncle. Together they supported his weight and helped him to a bed in the boat's small cabin.

"You kids will have to take over," he said. "I'll give you instructions, but it's up to you to sail us to shore."

Both Keesha and Shaun looked frightened. They had helped Uncle Ted sail the boat, but neither felt sure they could sail it alone.

"We'll just have to do it," said Keesha. "We've got to get Uncle Ted to a doctor as quickly as possible."

Looking out across the miles of dark blue water, the two could barely see the coastal mountains. Keesha steered the boat in that direction, while Shaun took care of the sails. Luckily, there was a steady wind, and in just a few hours, they were pulling into San Diego Harbor. Keesha jumped off the boat and tied it to the dock. Quickly, she found a police officer, who called an ambulance to help Uncle Ted.

Finally, as Uncle Ted was helped onto a stretcher, he told Keesha and Shaun, "I'm very lucky to have had two courageous mates aboard. I owe you a lot, including the remainder of our sailing trip!"

"That can wait," Keesha and Shaun said together, laughing.

1. What happened just after Keesha, Shaun, and Uncle Ted sailed out of Long Beach?
   ○ **A.** They had a problem with the mainsail.
   ○ **B.** They set sail for San Diego.
   ○ **C.** Uncle Ted fell and hurt himself.
   ○ **D.** They stopped for a while on Catalina Island.

2. What happened just before Uncle Ted fell to the deck?
   ○ **F.** Keesha and Shaun rushed to help him.
   ○ **G.** The mainsail became caught in the rigging.
   ○ **H.** A gust of wind rocked the boat.
   ○ **J.** Keesha took over steering the boat.

3. What event caused Keesha and Shaun to look frightened?
   ○ **A.** A gust of wind rocked the boat.
   ○ **B.** Uncle Ted asked them to take over sailing the boat.
   ○ **C.** Keesha could barely see the coastal mountains.
   ○ **D.** Uncle Ted named his boat the *Sea Gull*.

4. What did Keesha do as soon as she jumped off the boat and tied it up?
   ○ **F.** She asked a police officer to call an ambulance.
   ○ **G.** She helped Uncle Ted onto a stretcher.
   ○ **H.** She steered the boat toward San Diego.
   ○ **J.** She said she couldn't wait to finish the trip.

5. What clues does the author give about the sequence of events?
   ○ **A.** She uses dialogue to show who is speaking throughout the story.
   ○ **B.** She describes the weather at certain points in the action.
   ○ **C.** She uses time words and describes the events in order.
   ○ **D.** She lets the reader know something about each character.

Name _____

Predicting Outcomes

Read the passage and answer the questions that follow. Fill in the circle next to the best answer.

Going Camping

Jess was excited. This was his first camping trip with the Outdoor Club. Mr. Cruz, the club leader, had told Jess exactly what to bring along. Jess had packed everything on the list, plus a few more things he thought he might need to camp out.

At the campsite, the group members hurried to set things up. Jess picked out a flat spot for his tent. He bent down to hammer in one of the stakes and noticed a large footprint in the soft ground. "That looks like the footprint of a really large raccoon," he thought. He was just about to show Mr. Cruz, when the clanging dinner bell captured his attention. Jess made his way to the campfire and sat down with the others.

"As good as this food smells to us," said Mr. Cruz, "it smells even better to the bears. Remember, never leave food out around camp. We must keep all food locked in the car. That way, we won't tempt the bears." Just then, the group heard a roar far up the mountain. The noise emphasized Mr. Cruz's point.

After dinner, Jess and the others finished setting up their tents. It was late when Jess finally crawled inside. He opened his backpack to pull out his pajamas. There, on top of his clothes, was a box of snacks he had packed. Jess remembered Mr. Cruz's warning, but he figured that keeping the wrapped snacks would be all right. He crawled into his sleeping bag and dozed off.

Later, Jess awoke to a scratching noise outside his tent. He sat up and pulled back the tent flap. There, just to the side of Jess's tent, was a large bear. "It must have smelled the snacks!" Jess thought. Just as Jess yelled out for Mr. Cruz, the bear turned and began walking toward the open flap.

A fast-thinking Mr. Cruz came to the rescue. He quickly grabbed a large cooking pot and a spoon and began banging loudly. The sound scared the bear away. By now, all the campers were awake, and Jess had a lot of explaining to do.

Go on ⇨

1. What does Jess's sighting of the large footprint help you predict?
   - ○ **A.** Jess will learn how to identify many animals.
   - ○ **B.** A large animal might play a part in the story.
   - ○ **C.** The campers will not run into any other people.
   - ○ **D.** Jess and the others might discover a new kind of animal.

2. What clues help you predict that the footprint might belong to a bear?
   - ○ **F.** strange noises and the good-smelling food
   - ○ **G.** the clanging dinner bell and people around the campfire
   - ○ **H.** a locked car and empty tents
   - ○ **J.** Mr. Cruz's warning and the distant roar

3. What event makes you think Jess might run into trouble?
   - ○ **A.** Jess keeps the snacks he finds in his backpack.
   - ○ **B.** Jess finishes setting up his tent.
   - ○ **C.** Jess pulls his pajamas out of his backpack.
   - ○ **D.** Jess crawls into his sleeping bag and goes to sleep.

4. What will Mr. Cruz probably do after scaring the bear away?
   - ○ **F.** leave food in the woods to keep bears away from the tents
   - ○ **G.** gather the campers to chase after the bear
   - ○ **H.** ask Jess to lock his snacks in the car
   - ○ **J.** buy a bigger cooking pot and spoon

5. The next time Jess goes camping, what will he probably do?
   - ○ **A.** lock any food in the car
   - ○ **B.** eat his food all at once
   - ○ **C.** keep his tent flap closed
   - ○ **D.** feed the bears

Information and Study Skills

Read each question about the parts of a book. Fill in the circle next to the best answer.

1. In which part of a book will you find a list of chapters and the page numbers on which each begins?
   ○ **A.** table of contents   ○ **C.** title page
   ○ **B.** glossary   ○ **D.** index

2. What will you find in a bibliography?
   ○ **F.** names of the author, illustrator, and publisher
   ○ **G.** where and when the book was published
   ○ **H.** an alphabetical list of topics in the book
   ○ **J.** a list of sources the author used in writing the book

Read the following part of an index from a book about oceans. Then answer the question that follows. Fill in the circle next to the best answer.

Seaweeds, 66, 96	Shearwaters, 68, 69
Self-protection, 42	Shrimps, 76
Senses and sensors, 52–53	Snails, 120
Sewage, 82	
Sharks, 35, 42, 74, 105, 107	
hammerhead, 73	
mako, 32	
whale, 32	

3. Under which entry might you find information about how pollution affects the oceans?
   ○ **A.** Seaweeds   ○ **C.** Sewage
   ○ **B.** Senses and sensors   ○ **D.** Shrimps

Look at the chart and answer the questions that follow. Fill in the circle next to the best answer.

Voyages of Henry Hudson, 1607–1611		
Years	Starting Point	Destination
1607	England	England
1608	England	England
1609	Amsterdam, Holland	England
1610–1611	England	Hudson Bay, Canada

4. In what year did Hudson depart from Amsterdam?

   ○ **F.** 1607

   ○ **G.** 1608

   ○ **H.** 1609

   ○ **J.** 1610

5. Which part of the world did Hudson reach on his fourth and final voyage?

   ○ **A.** Holland

   ○ **B.** Canada

   ○ **C.** United States

   ○ **D.** England

Suffixes *-ful*, *-less*, and *-ly*

Read each sentence. Then find the meaning of the underlined word. Fill in the circle next to the best answer.

1. The children were <u>fearful</u> when they heard the loud clap of thunder.
   - ○ **A.** without fear
   - ○ **B.** in a way that causes fear
   - ○ **C.** full of fear
   - ○ **D.** able to feel fear

2. Mark felt <u>hopeless</u> as he looked across the flooded river at the stranded calf.
   - ○ **F.** without hope
   - ○ **G.** in a way that causes hope
   - ○ **H.** able to hope
   - ○ **J.** full of hope

3. The volunteers worked <u>rapidly</u> to finish the dam before the rains began.
   - ○ **A.** having no need to be rapid
   - ○ **B.** able to be rapid
   - ○ **C.** without being rapid
   - ○ **D.** in a way that is rapid

4. Alice spent several <u>sleepless</u> nights worrying about her missing dog.
   - ○ **F.** full of sleep
   - ○ **G.** without sleep
   - ○ **H.** able to have sleep
   - ○ **J.** in a sleepy way

5. The <u>flavorful</u> berries helped the lost campers survive until they were rescued.
   - ○ **A.** used as a flavoring
   - ○ **B.** without flavor
   - ○ **C.** able to give flavor
   - ○ **D.** full of flavor

Name _____

Syllabication

Read each sentence. Choose the correct way to divide the underlined word into syllables. Fill in the circle next to the best answer.

1. Jorge read the <u>cartoon</u> and then laughed out loud.

 ○ **A.** ca•rtoon
 ○ **B.** car•toon
 ○ **C.** cart•oon
 ○ **D.** carto•on

2. Anna bowed before the queen, as was the country's <u>custom</u>.

 ○ **F.** cu•stom
 ○ **G.** cust•om
 ○ **H.** cus•tom
 ○ **J.** custo•m

3. The tracks in the dirt were <u>evidence</u> that deer had been in the area.

 ○ **A.** ev•i•dence
 ○ **B.** evid•ence
 ○ **C.** e•vi•dence
 ○ **D.** ev•id•ence

4. The tired boys took a <u>refreshing</u> swim in the pool.

 ○ **F.** ref•res•hing
 ○ **G.** re•fres•hing
 ○ **H.** ref•resh•ing
 ○ **J.** re•fresh•ing

5. The captain of the ship tried to <u>navigate</u> slowly through the rocks.

 ○ **A.** na•vig•ate
 ○ **B.** nav•i•gate
 ○ **C.** navig•ate
 ○ **D.** na•vi•gate

Prefixes *un-* and *re-*

Read each sentence. Then find the meaning of the underlined word. Fill in the circle next to the best answer.

1. Heavy rains caused the family to <u>rethink</u> their plans to go on a picnic.
   - ○ **A.** not think
   - ○ **B.** think less
   - ○ **C.** think wrongly
   - ○ **D.** think again

2. All five campers were <u>uncomfortable</u> in the small, cramped tent.
   - ○ **F.** not comfortable
   - ○ **G.** comfortable again
   - ○ **H.** more comfortable
   - ○ **J.** in a comfortable way

3. The young babysitter fought to <u>regain</u> control over the roomful of excited children.
   - ○ **A.** gain again
   - ○ **B.** wrongly gain
   - ○ **C.** not gain
   - ○ **D.** gain in advance

4. Amazingly, the crew's lost boat appeared <u>unchanged</u> after twenty years.
   - ○ **F.** changed a lot
   - ○ **G.** changed again
   - ○ **H.** not changed
   - ○ **J.** more changed

5. The farmer spent weeks <u>rebuilding</u> his barn after the storm.
   - ○ **A.** not building
   - ○ **B.** building again
   - ○ **C.** building around
   - ○ **D.** building later

STOP

Name _____

Possessives and Contractions

Choose the words that correctly replace the underlined part of each sentence. Fill in the circle next to the best answer.

1. The map to Mirror Lake fell out of <u>the guide's backpack</u>.
    - ○ **A.** the backpack of the guides
    - ○ **B.** the backpack of the guide
    - ○ **C.** the guide and the backpack
    - ○ **D.** the guide of the backpack

2. Rita <u>couldn't</u> see the stars through the thick clouds.
    - ○ **F.** could not
    - ○ **G.** could have
    - ○ **H.** could be
    - ○ **J.** could never

3. "You <u>won't</u> believe how many trees are down," said Aunt Linda.
    - ○ **A.** would not
    - ○ **B.** will not
    - ○ **C.** will have
    - ○ **D.** would have

4. <u>The Smiths' neighbors</u> offered to help them move their furniture.
    - ○ **F.** the neighbors of Smith
    - ○ **G.** the Smiths and their neighbors
    - ○ **H.** the Smiths or their neighbors
    - ○ **J.** the neighbors of the Smiths

5. "You <u>shouldn't</u> talk on the phone during a lightning storm," said Grandma.
    - ○ **A.** should never
    - ○ **B.** should have
    - ○ **C.** should not
    - ○ **D.** should be

STOP

Name _____

Spelling

Find the correctly spelled word to complete each sentence.
Fill in the circle beside your answer.

1. Meg needed materials for her _____ project.
   - ○ **A.** creft
   - ○ **B.** craftt
   - ○ **C.** crafft
   - ○ **D.** craft

2. Her project had flowers and other plants as its _____.
   - ○ **F.** theem
   - ○ **G.** theeme
   - ○ **H.** theme
   - ○ **J.** theam

3. Meg would _____ to do her very best on the project.
   - ○ **A.** strive
   - ○ **B.** striv
   - ○ **C.** strieve
   - ○ **D.** stryve

4. She began to _____ the woods in her backyard.
   - ○ **F.** romme
   - ○ **G.** roam
   - ○ **H.** raom
   - ○ **J.** rhome

5. Meg spotted a lovely pink _____ beneath some bushes.
   - ○ **A.** bloum
   - ○ **B.** blume
   - ○ **C.** blome
   - ○ **D.** bloom

6. A _____ of pain crossed her face when a thorn suddenly pricked her arm.

- ○ **F.** wince
- ○ **G.** wence
- ○ **H.** winse
- ○ **J.** wiins

7. She _____ to remove it without ripping her shirt.

- ○ **A.** soght
- ○ **B.** sought
- ○ **C.** saught
- ○ **D.** sawght

8. Meg pulled the thorn back and forth in a regular _____.

- ○ **F.** rhythm
- ○ **G.** rhithm
- ○ **H.** rhethm
- ○ **J.** rythym

9. It would _____ Meg if she got a torn shirt and no flower!

- ○ **A.** annoi
- ○ **B.** annoie
- ○ **C.** annoy
- ○ **D.** anoy

10. In the end, she could not _____ getting a small rip in her shirt.

- ○ **F.** avoyd
- ○ **G.** avoid
- ○ **H.** avoyed
- ○ **J.** avode

Name _____

Vocabulary

Read each sentence. Then find the meaning of the underlined word. Fill in the circle next to the best answer.

1. The tourist did not have local <u>currency</u>, so he could not buy anything at the market.
    - ○ **A.** money
    - ○ **B.** clothes
    - ○ **C.** friends
    - ○ **D.** directions

2. All the campers were wet after being caught outside in the <u>drenching</u> rain.
    - ○ **F.** soaking
    - ○ **G.** freezing
    - ○ **H.** distant
    - ○ **J.** light

3. The carpenter made <u>precise</u> measurements, so all the table parts fit together perfectly.
    - ○ **A.** careless
    - ○ **B.** few
    - ○ **C.** exact
    - ○ **D.** numerous

Read each sentence. Then find the word that is in the same word family as the underlined word. Fill in the circle next to the best answer.

4. Everyone clapped when the <u>actor</u> appeared on the stage.
    - ○ **F.** theater
    - ○ **G.** action
    - ○ **H.** assistant
    - ○ **J.** play

5. The four students were rewarded for performing many hours of community <u>service</u>.
    - ○ **A.** volunteer
    - ○ **B.** certain
    - ○ **C.** personal
    - ○ **D.** servant

6. When Joe looked at the <u>thermometer</u>, he could not believe how hot it was.

   ◯ **F.** weather   ◯ **H.** thirsty

   ◯ **G.** thermos   ◯ **J.** instrument

Read the dictionary entry. Then read each question. Fill in the circle next to the best answer.

---

both•er (**bŏth′** ər) *v.* **both•ered, both•er•ing, both•ers. 1.** To disturb or anger; annoy: *Noise in the hall bothered the teacher.* **2.** To puzzle: *A problem had been bothering them.*

---

7. What part of speech is shown in the above dictionary entry?

   ◯ **A.** noun

   ◯ **B.** adjective

   ◯ **C.** pronunciation

   ◯ **D.** verb

8. Which of the following is the entry word from the above dictionary entry?

   ◯ **F.** (**bŏth′** ər)

   ◯ **G.** To disturb or anger; annoy

   ◯ **H.** **both•er**

   ◯ **J.** **both•er•ing**

Read each sentence. Fill in the circle next to the best answer.

9. Which of these words would you find on a dictionary page with the guide words *leader* and *lease*?

   ◯ **A.** leaf   ◯ **C.** least

   ◯ **B.** lapel   ◯ **D.** length

10. Which of these words comes first in a dictionary?

   ◯ **F.** rascal   ◯ **H.** rainfall

   ◯ **G.** rainbow   ◯ **J.** ramble

STOP

Name _____

Grammar

Read each sentence. Fill in the circle next to the best answer.

1. Which of these is an imperative sentence?
   - ○ **A.** Did you hit the ball?
   - ○ **B.** I want you to hit the ball.
   - ○ **C.** Hit the ball.
   - ○ **D.** I'm so glad you hit the ball!

2. Which of these is an interrogative sentence?
   - ○ **F.** Did you do your chores?
   - ○ **G.** I see that you did your chores.
   - ○ **H.** Please do your chores.
   - ○ **J.** You did your chores so quickly!

3. Which choice shows the simple subject in the following sentence?

   The busy volunteers built the house in just one week.
   - ○ **A.** The busy volunteers
   - ○ **B.** volunteers
   - ○ **C.** the house
   - ○ **D.** built

4. Which choice shows the complete predicate in the following sentence?

   The grateful family could not wait to move in.
   - ○ **F.** could not wait
   - ○ **G.** The grateful family
   - ○ **H.** to move in
   - ○ **J.** could not wait to move in

5. Which choice correctly combines the following two sentences into a compound sentence?

The volunteers had many different skills. Working together made the job go faster.

- ○ **A.** Because the volunteers had many different skills, working together made the job go faster.
- ○ **B.** The volunteers had many different skills working together, and made the job go faster.
- ○ **C.** The volunteers, working together with many different skills, made the job go faster.
- ○ **D.** The volunteers had many different skills, and working together made the job go faster.

6. Which choice correctly combines the following two sentences into a complex sentence?

The weather became cold and damp. The volunteers continued to work.

- ○ **F.** The weather became cold and damp, but the volunteers continued to work.
- ○ **G.** The volunteers continued to work in the cold, damp weather.
- ○ **H.** Although the weather became cold and damp, the volunteers continued to work.
- ○ **J.** In the cold, damp weather, the volunteers continued to work.

7. Which of these is **not** a sentence fragment?

- ○ **A.** Many busy workers and with their own tools.
- ○ **B.** Many busy workers had come with their own tools.
- ○ **C.** All day, many busy workers with their own tools.
- ○ **D.** With their own tools, many busy workers.

8. In which sentence are proper nouns capitalized correctly?

- ○ **F.** My Uncle and judge Mary Brown did most of the electrical wiring.
- ○ **G.** My uncle and Judge Mary Brown did most of the Electrical wiring.
- ○ **H.** My uncle and Judge mary brown did most of the electrical wiring.
- ○ **J.** My uncle and Judge Mary Brown did most of the electrical wiring.

Go on ▷

9. In which sentence are proper nouns capitalized correctly?

   ○ **A.** Reporters from the neighboring towns of Smithville and Jonestown, iowa, wrote Articles about the project.

   ○ **B.** Reporters from the neighboring towns of smithville and jonestown, Iowa, wrote articles about the Project.

   ○ **C.** Reporters from the neighboring towns of Smithville and Jonestown, Iowa, wrote articles about the project.

   ○ **D.** Reporters from the neighboring Towns of smithville and jonestown, Iowa, wrote Articles about the Project.

10. Which sentence has the correct plural forms of nouns?

   ○ **F.** Mans, womans, and childs in cities everywhere can volunteer.

   ○ **G.** Men, women, and childs in citys everywhere can volunteer.

   ○ **H.** Men, women, and children in cities everywhere can volunteer.

   ○ **J.** Mens, womens, and childrens in cities everywhere can volunteer.

Name _____

Writing Skills

Find the sentence that uses sequence words or phrases most clearly. Fill in the circle next to the best answer.

1. ○ **A.** Mrs. Carter called on Joan next, and first she called on Treena.
   ○ **B.** Mrs. Carter called on Joan last, and then she called on Treena.
   ○ **C.** Mrs. Carter called on Joan first, and then she called on Treena.
   ○ **D.** Mrs. Carter called on Joan then, and first she called on Treena.

Find the sentence that has no errors in capitalization or punctuation. Fill in the circle next to the best answer.

2. ○ **F.** my friend Chan is taking the plane to Orlando, Florida
   ○ **G.** my friend Chan is taking the plane to Orlando, Florida.
   ○ **H.** My friend Chan is taking the plane to Orlando, Florida.
   ○ **J.** My friend Chan is taking the plane to Orlando, Florida

3. ○ **A.** Did you visit the baseball park when you were in Houston?
   ○ **B.** Did you visit the baseball park when you were in Houston
   ○ **C.** Did you visit the baseball park when you were in Houston.
   ○ **D.** did you visit the baseball park when you were in Houston?

Read each pair of sentences. Then choose the best way to combine them into a sentence with an appositive. Fill in the circle next to the best answer.

4. Mrs. Lopez opened the assembly with a speech. Mrs. Lopez is our principal.

   ○ **F.** Mrs. Lopez is our principal, and she opened the assembly with a speech.

   ○ **G.** Mrs. Lopez, our principal, opened the assembly with a speech.

   ○ **H.** Our principal is Mrs. Lopez, and she opened the assembly with a speech.

   ○ **J.** Opening the assembly with a speech, our principal is Mrs. Lopez.

5. Premier Pictures is going to close in June. Premier Pictures is the only movie theater in town.

   ○ **A.** Although it is the only movie theater in town, Premier Pictures is going to close in June.

   ○ **B.** Premier Pictures is the only movie theater in town, and it is going to close in June.

   ○ **C.** Premier Pictures is going to close in June, and it is the only movie theater in town.

   ○ **D.** Premier Pictures, the only movie theater in town, is going to close in June.

What Really Happened?

Level 6, Theme 2
Theme Skills Test Record

Student _____ Date _____

Student Record Form	Possible Score	Criterion Score	Student Score
Part A: Fact and Opinion	5	4	
Part B: Making Inferences	5	4	
Part C: Text Organization	5	4	
Part D: Information and Study Skills	5	4	
Part E: "Someone Who" Suffixes	5	4	
Part F: Inflected Endings -s, -es	5	4	
Part G: Adjective Suffixes -al, -ive, -ous	5	4	
Part H: Spelling	10	8	
Part I: Vocabulary	10	8	
Part J: Grammar	10	8	
Part K: Writing Skills	5	4	
TOTAL	70	56	
		Total Student Score x 1.43 =	%

Name _____

Fact and Opinion

Read the passage and answer the questions that follow. Fill in the circle next to the best answer.

Benjamin Franklin

Benjamin Franklin is one of America's most important figures. He was born in 1706 in Boston, seventy years before the United States gained independence. He grew up in a large family. In fact, he was the fifteenth of seventeen children! Franklin went to school for only two years. He learned mainly by reading books and studying on his own.

Franklin hated delays and untidiness. He felt that all tasks should be done as quickly as possible. Each morning he wrote two admirable traits in his diary, such as generosity and kindness. Then he would try to practice those traits all day. This is why Franklin became such a fine person.

At the age of twelve, Franklin began working as a printer. He and his older brother published the *New England Courant,* one of the first newspapers in North America. Perhaps his early experience as a printer prepared Franklin for his career in publishing. He bought a newspaper, the *Pennsylvania Gazette,* in 1729. Then in the 1730s he began publishing *Poor Richard's Almanack.* This was a booklet of practical advice and witty sayings. Franklin may be best known for his sayings. One of these is "Early to bed and early to rise, makes a man healthy, wealthy, and wise."

Franklin was very interested in science. His most famous experiment, by far, was flying a kite in a thunderstorm. By doing this he proved that lightning was a form of electricity. Franklin also invented many things. His best inventions were bifocal glasses, lightning rods, and the Franklin stove.

In later life, Franklin served his country as deputy Postmaster General. He held this position for twenty-one years. Then in 1776 Franklin helped to write the Declaration of Independence. He also worked on the treaty that ended the Revolutionary War. Finally, he helped to write the United States Constitution when he was eighty-one years old. This was Franklin's greatest accomplishment.

Go on ⟹

1. Which of the following is an opinion?

   ○ **A.** Benjamin Franklin is one of America's most important figures.
   ○ **B.** Benjamin Franklin was born in 1706 in Boston.
   ○ **C.** Benjamin Franklin grew up in a large family.
   ○ **D.** Benjamin Franklin went to school for only two years.

2. Which of the following **can** be proved?

   ○ **F.** Franklin hated delays and untidiness.
   ○ **G.** Franklin felt that all tasks should be done as quickly as possible.
   ○ **H.** Each morning Franklin wrote two admirable traits in his diary.
   ○ **J.** This is why Franklin became such a fine person.

3. Which word in the sentence signals that it is an opinion?

   Perhaps his early experience as a printer prepared Franklin for his career in publishing.

   ○ **A.** Perhaps
   ○ **B.** early
   ○ **C.** experience
   ○ **D.** prepared

4. Which statement from the passage is a fact?

   ○ **F.** Franklin may be best known for his sayings.
   ○ **G.** Franklin proved that lightning was a form of electricity.
   ○ **H.** Franklin's most famous experiment, by far, was flying a kite in a thunderstorm.
   ○ **J.** Franklin's best inventions were bifocal glasses and the Franklin stove.

5. Which detail from the last paragraph is impossible to prove?

   ○ **A.** Franklin served his country as deputy Postmaster General.
   ○ **B.** Franklin held this position for twenty-one years.
   ○ **C.** Franklin helped to write the United States Constitution.
   ○ **D.** This was Franklin's greatest accomplishment.

Name _____

Making Inferences

Read the passage and answer the questions that follow. Fill in the circle next to the best answer.

The Pony Express

The Pony Express began in 1860. Its purpose was to deliver mail quickly. Mail was carried between St. Joseph, Missouri, and Sacramento, California. The other major mail carrier, Wells Fargo, took about twenty days to get mail from one place to the next. By offering quicker service, the Pony Express owners hoped to gain large mail-delivery contracts.

Three men in the stagecoach business came up with the idea for the Pony Express. They bought 600 well-trained broncos, chosen for their speed and strength. Then they hired seventy-five riders. The riders were selected for their bravery and their knowledge of horses. They were also chosen for their size. Small, skinny riders were preferred.

The first Pony Express rider was Henry Wallace. He set out from St. Joseph on April 3, 1860. He carried in his saddlebag a message from President Buchanan to the Governor of California. The message had been telegraphed to St. Joseph just that morning.

The package that Wallace carried out of St. Joseph reached Sacramento in just ten days. It was carried without a stop between the two cities. Each rider rode at top speed for 75 to 100 miles. During this time, the rider changed horses six times at relay stops. At the end of one rider's run, the saddlebags were handed off to the next rider. Then the process began again.

The Pony Express offered a valuable service, but it lasted for less than two years. Along the Pony Express route, railroads were being built. Soon trains would travel from coast to coast. Even ahead of the railroads, telegraph wires were being strung. When the first telegraph line reached California, the Pony Express no longer existed.

1. From the first paragraph, what can you infer about Sacramento, California?
   - ○ **A.** Sacramento was very close to St. Joseph.
   - ○ **B.** People would rather send mail to Sacramento than visit there.
   - ○ **C.** Sacramento was a great distance from St. Joseph.
   - ○ **D.** People who lived in Sacramento seldom received mail.

2. Why were Pony Express riders chosen for their small size?
   - ○ **F.** A horse could run faster with a light rider.
   - ○ **G.** Light riders could easily jump from one horse to the next.
   - ○ **H.** Light riders tended to eat less along the trail.
   - ○ **J.** Saddlebags fit more easily on a light rider.

3. Based on the third paragraph, what can you infer about long-distance communication in 1860?
   - ○ **A.** All people found it difficult to communicate with one another over long distances.
   - ○ **B.** Telegraph communications were possible between Washington, D.C., and St. Joseph.
   - ○ **C.** Important people preferred writing letters to sending telegraphs.
   - ○ **D.** The President did not like to talk with governors of distant states.

4. Based on the fourth paragraph, what can you infer about the horses?
   - ○ **F.** They could run faster than the Wells Fargo horses.
   - ○ **G.** They could run at top speed for only a short while.
   - ○ **H.** They did not like to have saddlebags attached to their saddles.
   - ○ **J.** There were certain riders they preferred to carry.

5. What can you infer from the last sentence?
   - ○ **A.** Pony Express riders could not travel along the trails where telegraph lines were strung.
   - ○ **B.** The riders wanted to work for the telegraph company instead of for the Pony Express.
   - ○ **C.** The first telegraph message told people in California that they were being overcharged by the Pony Express riders.
   - ○ **D.** The Pony Express could not compete with the speed and convenience of telegraph communications.

STOP

Name _____

Text Organization

Read the passage and answer the questions that follow. Fill in the circle next to the best answer.

How Dolphins Use Sound

Dolphins, like humans, are mammals. Unlike most mammals, though, dolphins live in the oceans. One of the most interesting things about dolphins is the way they use sound. Sound helps them exist in their watery environment in a variety of ways.

Using Sound to See

Dolphins use sound to help them create visual images in dark waters. A dolphin sends out regular pulses of sound. These sounds bounce off any object they come in contact with. Then the sounds echo back to the dolphin. These echoes are transformed in the dolphin's brain into a sound picture of the dolphin's surroundings.

Making Many Different Sounds

Dolphins make many different sounds. Each dolphin has a special sound that distinguishes it from others. By sending out this special sound, a dolphin can identify itself. Dolphin sounds have been described as whistles, clicks, and creaks. The clicks and creaks sound much like a squeaky door hinge. Dolphins can make up to 300 clicking sounds each second. In fact, they make sounds at many different speeds and at varying noise levels. Scientists have studied these sounds, but they have not found any regular patterns. They cannot prove that dolphins use sounds to communicate in a way similar to people.

Using Sound as a Weapon

Strangely, dolphins can use sound as a weapon. They send a strong, focused burst of sound out toward their prey. The sound stuns small creatures in the sound's path. In this way, dolphins can easily catch the fish that make up their diet.

1. How has the author organized the passage?
   - ○ **A.** telling a story
   - ○ **B.** sequence of events
   - ○ **C.** cause and effect
   - ○ **D.** main ideas and details

2. What is the passage mainly about?
   - ○ **F.** the daily life of dolphins
   - ○ **G.** how dolphins use sound
   - ○ **H.** the many different sounds dolphins make
   - ○ **J.** using sound as a weapon

3. Which of the following is a detail supporting the idea that dolphins make many different sounds?
   - ○ **A.** The clicks and squeaks sound like a squeaky door hinge.
   - ○ **B.** Sound echoes are transformed in the dolphin's brain into sound pictures.
   - ○ **C.** Unlike most mammals, dolphins live in the ocean.
   - ○ **D.** Dolphins send out focused bursts of sound toward their prey.

4. Which of the following is **not** a main idea in the passage?
   - ○ **F.** Dolphins use sound to help them see.
   - ○ **G.** Dolphins send out regular pulses of sound.
   - ○ **H.** Dolphins make many different sounds.
   - ○ **J.** Dolphins use sound as a weapon.

5. How does the author help you focus on the main ideas?
   - ○ **A.** by comparing dolphins to humans
   - ○ **B.** by proving that dolphins use sound to communicate
   - ○ **C.** by using headings
   - ○ **D.** by giving examples of dolphin sounds

Name _____

Information and Study Skills

Review the reference sources in the table below. Then answer the questions that follow. Fill in the circle next to the best answer.

Reference Source	What It Contains
Almanac	Brief, up-to-date facts about governments, sports events, countries, and subjects of general interest
Atlas	Maps and an index that tells where to find maps of various places
Dictionary	Alphabetized listing of words, including their spelling, pronunciation, meaning, and sometimes their history
Encyclopedia	Summaries of major facts about a variety of subjects, which are listed alphabetically
Internet sites	Information found in most other reference sources
Telephone directory	Phone numbers for homes, businesses, and public agencies
Thesaurus	Synonyms and antonyms for commonly used words

Go on

1. If you wanted to find information about the moons of Jupiter, which reference source would you use?
   - ○ **A.** dictionary
   - ○ **B.** encyclopedia
   - ○ **C.** thesaurus
   - ○ **D.** atlas

2. To find the meaning of *implausible,* where would you look?
   - ○ **F.** dictionary
   - ○ **G.** encyclopedia
   - ○ **H.** atlas
   - ○ **J.** almanac

3. If you need to find out the population of Florida, which two reference sources could you use?
   - ○ **A.** telephone directory and dictionary
   - ○ **B.** encyclopedia and thesaurus
   - ○ **C.** dictionary and atlas
   - ○ **D.** almanac and Internet

4. If you want to learn which country is closer to the North Pole — France or Italy — where would you look?
   - ○ **F.** thesaurus
   - ○ **G.** almanac
   - ○ **H.** atlas
   - ○ **J.** dictionary

5. If you need to find a word to use in place of *ask*, where would you look?
   - ○ **A.** thesaurus
   - ○ **B.** encyclopedia
   - ○ **C.** atlas
   - ○ **D.** telephone directory

"Someone Who" Suffixes

Read each sentence below and answer the question that follows it. Fill in the circle next to the best answer.

1. *The young pianist walked onto the stage and smiled at her teacher and the conductor.*

   Which word means "someone who plays the piano"?
   - ○ **A.** pianist
   - ○ **B.** stage
   - ○ **C.** teacher
   - ○ **D.** conductor

2. *The teachers and volunteers hung the paintings while students finished their collages.*

   Which word means "those who study"?
   - ○ **F.** teachers
   - ○ **G.** volunteers
   - ○ **H.** paintings
   - ○ **J.** students

3. *A translator helped the traveler request a song from the music director and the musician.*

   Which word means "someone who plays music"?
   - ○ **A.** translator
   - ○ **B.** traveler
   - ○ **C.** director
   - ○ **D.** musician

4. *The merchant told the beggar that he needed a worker for his store.*

   Which word means "one who works"?
   - ○ **F.** merchant
   - ○ **G.** beggar
   - ○ **H.** worker
   - ○ **J.** store

5. *An assistant to the lawyer said she would be the interpreter for their clients.*

   Which word means "one who explains, or interprets, something"?
   - ○ **A.** assistant
   - ○ **B.** interpreter
   - ○ **C.** lawyer
   - ○ **D.** clients

Name _____

Inflected Endings -s, -es

Read each sentence. Then find the word that is made up of a base word and an ending. Fill in the circle next to the best answer.

1. Lewis and Clark were two famous explorers.
   ○ **A.** Lewis
   ○ **B.** Clark
   ○ **C.** famous
   ○ **D.** explorers

2. They could not guess what they might find in the spaces to the west.
   ○ **F.** guess
   ○ **G.** might
   ○ **H.** spaces
   ○ **J.** west

3. The two men had to cross many deep rivers and dark forests.
   ○ **A.** men
   ○ **B.** cross
   ○ **C.** many
   ○ **D.** rivers

4. They ate fresh berries and fish along with food they brought with them.
   ○ **F.** fish
   ○ **G.** berries
   ○ **H.** along
   ○ **J.** brought

5. Lewis and Clark became close friends with one special guide.
   ○ **A.** friends
   ○ **B.** close
   ○ **C.** became
   ○ **D.** special

STOP

Adjective Suffixes *-al, -ive, -ous*

Read each sentence. Then find the meaning of the underlined word. Fill in the circle next to the best answer.

1. The students enjoyed reading accounts of <u>historical</u> events.
   - ○ **A.** needing history
   - ○ **B.** not important in history
   - ○ **C.** relating to history
   - ○ **D.** lacking history

2. They cooked a feast and had a <u>joyous</u> celebration.
   - ○ **F.** without joy
   - ○ **G.** unable to have joy
   - ○ **H.** full of joy
   - ○ **J.** needing joy

3. Everyone agreed that Mac's arm needed <u>medical</u> attention.
   - ○ **A.** full of medicine
   - ○ **B.** relating to medicine
   - ○ **C.** containing medicine
   - ○ **D.** needing medicine

4. Jason found an <u>effective</u> way to get everyone involved.
   - ○ **F.** having a desired effect
   - ○ **G.** without any effect
   - ○ **H.** having the wrong effect
   - ○ **J.** having no effect

5. People passing by were <u>envious</u> of the settlers' camp.
   - ○ **A.** without envy
   - ○ **B.** unable to envy
   - ○ **C.** needing to envy
   - ○ **D.** full of envy

Name _____

Spelling

Find the correctly spelled word to complete each sentence. Fill in the circle beside your answer.

1. The _____ house sat in the middle of a green meadow.
    - ○ **A.** manner
    - ○ **B.** manor
    - ○ **C.** mannor
    - ○ **D.** maner

2. The new owners loved the _____ setting.
    - ○ **F.** rooral
    - ○ **G.** rurel
    - ○ **H.** reural
    - ○ **J.** rural

3. They liked to watch the birds _____ happily above the trees.
    - ○ **A.** whirl
    - ○ **B.** whurl
    - ○ **C.** wherl
    - ○ **D.** whirrl

4. Nothing seemed to _____ the swooping birds.
    - ○ **F.** frightn
    - ○ **G.** frightin
    - ○ **H.** frighten
    - ○ **J.** frightyn

5. One day, a _____ delivered an invitation to the new owners.
    - ○ **A.** mesenger
    - ○ **B.** messengyr
    - ○ **C.** messengir
    - ○ **D.** messenger

6. The royal family had _____ the invitation.

○ **F.** scent
○ **G.** cent
○ **H.** sent
○ **J.** sint

7. The family, _____ castle sat on a big hill, was throwing a party.

○ **A.** who's
○ **B.** whose
○ **C.** whos
○ **D.** whoos

8. Feeling nervous, the new owners decided to _____ what they would say.

○ **F.** rehearse
○ **G.** reherse
○ **H.** rehears
○ **J.** rehurse

9. Meanwhile, the queen's social _____ had everything under control.

○ **A.** directre
○ **B.** directer
○ **C.** director
○ **D.** directyr

10. She had planned many _____ events in the past.

○ **F.** similer
○ **G.** simaler
○ **H.** similor
○ **J.** similar

Name _____

Vocabulary

Find the correctly spelled word to complete each sentence. Fill in the circle next to the best answer.

1. Charisse let the bread _____ rise in the kitchen.
   - ○ **A.** doe
   - ○ **C.** dough
   - ○ **B.** dole
   - ○ **D.** due

2. The boy's _____ complexion led the nurse to believe he was sick.
   - ○ **F.** pole
   - ○ **H.** pal
   - ○ **G.** pale
   - ○ **J.** pail

3. "I cannot _____ my left shoe," complained Maria.
   - ○ **A.** find
   - ○ **C.** finned
   - ○ **B.** fined
   - ○ **D.** fine

4. Jason has the starring _____ in the school play.
   - ○ **F.** rule
   - ○ **H.** roll
   - ○ **G.** rail
   - ○ **J.** role

Read each dictionary entry. Then choose the word in which the syllables are stressed correctly. Fill in the circle next to the best answer.

5. **ad•ver•tise** (ăd′ vər tīz′) *v.* To call public attention to a product or business.
   - ○ **A.** ad•VER•tise
   - ○ **C.** AD•ver•tise
   - ○ **B.** AD•VER•tise
   - ○ **D.** ad•ver•TISE

6.   **per•form•ance** (pər fôr′ məns) *n.* A public presentation of something.

    ○ **F.** per•for•MANCE   ○ **H.** per•FOR•MANCE

    ○ **G.** PER•for•mance   ○ **J.** per•FOR•mance

7.   **ex•er•cise** (ĕk′ sər sīz′) *n.* An activity that requires great physical or mental effort.

    ○ **A.** EX•er•cise   ○ **C.** EX•ER•cise

    ○ **B.** ex•ER•cise   ○ **D.** ex•er•CISE

8.   **fab•u•lous** (făb′ yə ləs) *adj.* Barely believable; astonishing.

    ○ **F.** fab•U•lous   ○ **H.** FAB•u•lous

    ○ **G.** fab•u•LOUS   ○ **J.** FAB•u•LOUS

Look at this part of a spelling table/pronunciation key. Then answer the questions. Fill in the circle next to the best answer.

Sound	Spellings	Sample Words
/ā/	a, ai, ei, ey	m**a**de, pl**ai**t, v**ei**n, th**ey**
/ē/	e, ee, ie, y	th**e**se, fl**ee**t, ch**ie**f, bump**y**
/ō/	o, oe, ou, ow	f**o**ld, t**oe**, b**ou**lder, sl**ow**

9.   Which word has the same vowel sound as the sample word *slow*?

    ○ **A.** shoe   ○ **C.** cough

    ○ **B.** stolen   ○ **D.** luck

10.   What are possible spellings of the /ē/ sound?

    ○ **F.** o, u, ou, oo   ○ **H.** o, oe, ou, ow

    ○ **G.** e, ee, ie, y   ○ **J.** a, ai, ei, ey

J   Name _____

Grammar

Read each sentence. Fill in the circle next to the best answer.

1. Complete the sentence with the correct possessive noun.

   The _____ laughter filled the house.

   ○ **A.** childrens   ○ **C.** children's
   ○ **B.** childrens'   ○ **D.** childrens's

2. Complete the sentence with an action verb and a direct object.

   When the game began, Judy _____.

   ○ **F.** hit the ball
   ○ **G.** was excited
   ○ **H.** watched and clapped
   ○ **J.** ran inside

3. Find the sentence that has a main verb and an auxiliary verb.

   ○ **A.** Amanda was in the garden yesterday.
   ○ **B.** She pulled weeds from the flower beds.
   ○ **C.** A frog jumped out and surprised her.
   ○ **D.** She had moved his favorite rock.

4. Find the sentence that has a transitive verb.

   ○ **F.** Jimmy walked slowly along the path.
   ○ **G.** He playfully kicked a stone as he walked along.
   ○ **H.** He was happy to be outside on such a day.
   ○ **J.** Summer was always his favorite time of year.

5. Find the sentence that has a linking verb.

   ○ **A.** Sam is in a great mood.
   ○ **B.** He and his friends are on a baseball team.
   ○ **C.** Sam is happy when the game starts.
   ○ **D.** His sister Ann is in the stands.

6. Complete the sentence with the correct possessive noun.

Both _____ uniforms were lost before the game.

○ **F.** team's

○ **G.** teams

○ **H.** teams'

○ **J.** teams's

7. Complete the sentence with an action verb and a direct object.

I had just enough money, so I _____.

○ **A.** went to the game

○ **B.** was one of the fans at the game

○ **C.** sat in the best seat

○ **D.** bought a ticket to the game

8. Find the sentence in which the main verb is underlined.

○ **F.** The girls will <u>swim</u> in the pool later.

○ **G.** The lifeguard <u>has</u> gone on a break right now.

○ **H.** Everyone <u>was</u> playing noisily beside the pool.

○ **J.** Joe <u>will</u> jump off the diving board first.

9. Find the sentence that has an intransitive verb.

○ **A.** All the friends flew kites in the kite-flying contest.

○ **B.** Mari, the youngest, was the winner.

○ **C.** The wind blew the kites higher and higher.

○ **D.** She proudly showed her ribbon to everyone.

10. Find the sentence that has a linking verb and a predicate adjective.

○ **F.** Lalo kicked his shoes off.

○ **G.** He ran around in the soft grass.

○ **H.** The boy with Lalo was Jaime.

○ **J.** Jaime was glad to be Lalo's friend.

Name _____

Writing Skills

Read each sentence. Find the verb that makes the sentence most interesting and descriptive. Fill in the circle next to the best answer.

1. All at once, the two bears _____ into the woods.
   - ○ **A.** vanished
   - ○ **B.** ran
   - ○ **C.** walked
   - ○ **D.** went

2. The wind began to blow, and suddenly rain _____ from the sky.
   - ○ **F.** fell
   - ○ **G.** dropped
   - ○ **H.** came
   - ○ **J.** poured

3. The lovely ballerina _____ across the stage.
   - ○ **A.** floated
   - ○ **B.** danced
   - ○ **C.** moved
   - ○ **D.** walked

4. The hurdler cleared the last hurdle and _____ to the finish line.
   - ○ **F.** ran
   - ○ **G.** hurried
   - ○ **H.** dashed
   - ○ **J.** went

5. See how that stone _____ in the sunlight!
   - ○ **A.** shines
   - ○ **B.** sparkles
   - ○ **C.** appears
   - ○ **D.** looks

STOP

Growing Up

Level 6, Theme 3
Theme Skills Test Record

Student _____ Date _____

Student Record Form	Possible Score	Criterion Score	Student Score
Part A: Making Generalizations	5	4	
Part B: Making Inferences	5	4	
Part C: Story Structure	5	4	
Part D: Problem Solving and Decision Making	5	4	
Part E: Information and Study Skills	5	4	
Part F: VCV, VCCV, and VCCCV Patterns	5	4	
Part G: Words Ending in -ed or -ing	5	4	
Part H: Endings and Suffixes -en, -ize, -ify	5	4	
Part I: Prefixes in-, im-, and con-	5	4	
Part J: Spelling	10	8	
Part K: Vocabulary	10	8	
Part L: Grammar	10	8	
Part M: Writing Skills	5	4	
TOTAL	80	64	
		Total Student Score x 1.25 =	%

Name _____

Making Generalizations

Read the passage and answer the questions that follow. Fill in the circle next to the best answer.

Ready to Play

Sara had been practicing her flute every day for weeks. She knew she was prepared. Now that the band contest was here, though, Sara was feeling nervous. She wanted so badly to win a place in the first flute section. That would be the reward for all her hard work.

"Try to relax," Sara's friend Lisa said. "You know all your scales. You've memorized your solo, and you play it really well. You're going to do just fine!"

"Oh, I hope you're right," Sara sighed. "I drew number 34, and I probably won't get to play until late this afternoon. I wish I could have gone earlier," she said. "Judges always score harder when they're tired."

"Well, look at it this way. We've got some time, so let's go get something to eat," urged Lisa. "It will take your mind off the competition."

Sara and Lisa walked into the cafeteria and looked over the choices. Sara thought it was a good omen that they were serving her favorite thing — spaghetti with meatballs. She and Lisa filled their plates and found a table. Soon they were talking and laughing as they did on most school days.

"You were right, Lisa," said Sara. "Getting lunch and having some fun has helped me feel less nervous." She gave Lisa a quick hug. "A good friend is all a person needs to become a success."

Finally, the time came for Sara to perform. She walked into the judging room and, with shaking hands, placed her music on the stand. Then she took a deep breath and began to play. Soon, she was actually feeling relaxed. All the practice had paid off. Sara realized then that good preparation was the best medicine for a case of stage fright.

1. What generalization does this passage help you make about competing in contests?

   ○ **A.** People often get nervous just before a competition.
   ○ **B.** Practicing too much before a contest can make you nervous.
   ○ **C.** Most competitions offer no real rewards.
   ○ **D.** The person who really wants to win will get first place.

2. Which word in the following sentence signals that it is a generalization?

   Judges always score harder when they're tired.

   ○ **F.** Judges
   ○ **G.** always
   ○ **H.** harder
   ○ **J.** tired

3. Which sentence from the passage is an overgeneralization?

   ○ **A.** You've memorized your solo, and you play it really well.
   ○ **B.** You're going to do just fine.
   ○ **C.** It will take your mind off the competition.
   ○ **D.** A good friend is all a person needs to become a success.

4. After reading this passage, what generalization can you make about friendships?

   ○ **F.** Friends should not compete against each other.
   ○ **G.** Friends can help you work through your problems.
   ○ **H.** Friends tell you only what you want to hear.
   ○ **J.** Friends always like to do everything together.

5. Which word keeps the following sentence from being an overgeneralization?

   Being prepared often helps a performer feel confident.

   ○ **A.** prepared
   ○ **B.** helps
   ○ **C.** often
   ○ **D.** feel

Name _____

Making Inferences

Read the passage and answer the questions that follow. Fill in the circle next to the best answer.

A Surprising Visit

Josephine's mother joined her by the creek's edge. "I do *not* want to go visit your cousin," Josephine said to her mother. "Why can't I just stay here while you go?" She squatted near the water, examining a jar full of murky liquid.

"I know you don't have fun at Lallie's house," Josephine's mother said, "but I promised her a visit today. Her father is in town, and he's never met you. She'd be upset if you didn't come."

Josephine gave a long sigh. Then she poured out the creek water and followed her mother.

Lallie greeted them at the front gate. "I'm so glad you're here!" she cried. In the living room Aunt Lallie introduced Josephine to an elderly man with bushy white hair and rimless glasses. "This is your Great-uncle Morris."

The man sprang from his chair and said, "How do you do!"

"Why don't you two play checkers?" suggested Lallie.

As the two began a game of checkers, Josephine tried to think of something to say. She heard herself suddenly blurt out: "I saw a blotched water snake in the creek by my house this morning."

Morris peered at her. "No kidding — probably a *Nerodia erythrogaster transversa!*" he exclaimed. "They're rather rare around here."

Josephine looked at her great-uncle with amazement. "Do you know about snakes?" she asked.

"Of course — I'm a naturalist for the state museum. Nothing excites me more than finding a rare snake. Let's go take a look!"

Josephine and Morris spent the rest of the day exploring the snake's habitat — the local creek.

On the way home, Josephine thought to herself, "My great-uncle is a herpetologist. Cool!"

1. What can you infer about Josephine from the first three paragraphs?
   - ○ **A.** She does not usually obey her mother.
   - ○ **B.** She knows a lot about flowers, trees, and animals.
   - ○ **C.** She enjoys nature and being outdoors.
   - ○ **D.** She and her mother's cousin do not like each other.

2. How do you know that Josephine is trying to get along with Morris?
   - ○ **F.** She refuses to play checkers with her great-uncle.
   - ○ **G.** She looks at him with amazement.
   - ○ **H.** She tries to think of something to say.
   - ○ **J.** She finds it hard to smile.

3. Why do you think Josephine tells Morris about the water snake?
   - ○ **A.** She can't think of anything else to say to him.
   - ○ **B.** She plans to tell him all about it.
   - ○ **C.** She wants to find out if Morris knows anything about snakes.
   - ○ **D.** She wants to embarrass Morris.

4. Which of Morris's comments gets Josephine's attention?
   - ○ **F.** "I'm a naturalist for the state museum."
   - ○ **G.** "No kidding — probably a *Nerodia erythrogaster transversa!*"
   - ○ **H.** "Nothing excites me more than finding a rare snake."
   - ○ **J.** "Let's go take a look!"

5. Which clue tells you that Josephine has enjoyed her visit?
   - ○ **A.** She promises to write to her great-uncle.
   - ○ **B.** She doesn't want to leave Lallie's house.
   - ○ **C.** She goes home with her mother.
   - ○ **D.** She thinks it's cool that her great-uncle is a herpetologist.

Name _____

Story Structure

Read the passage and answer the questions that follow. Fill in the circle next to the best answer.

The Clubhouse

Ray woke up gradually, enjoying the warm summer morning. Then he sat up quickly. "How could I have forgotten!" he exclaimed. "Today's the day we build the clubhouse. Dustin and Arnie will be here any minute!" He rushed downstairs just in time to meet his friends at the front door. The three boys walked through the house and out into Ray's back yard. They had big plans for their new hideaway!

"It will be our secret place," said Arnie.

"We'll have a password," added Dustin.

"We can even sleep in it on warm nights," Ray chimed in. "Maybe we should make it a tree house."

The boys considered each of the backyard trees. The peach tree had limbs low enough to reach, but they weren't very sturdy. The oaks had strong limbs, but they were too high to reach from the ground.

"Maybe a tree house isn't such a good idea," said Ray. "My mom would never let us use the ladder to climb up there."

"What about a cabin?" suggested Arnie. "We could nail a bunch of boards together and make a cabin."

"Nope," said Dustin. "We don't have enough lumber to do anything like that." The boys plopped down onto the grass, each trying to come up with a good idea. Just then, they heard a truck pulling into the driveway.

"That must be our new refrigerator," said Ray. "It's supposed to be delivered today." The boys watched as the delivery men opened the bottom of a huge crate and carefully removed the new refrigerator. Ray's eyes lit up. "Are you thinking what I'm thinking?" he asked Arnie and Dustin. "That crate would make a perfect clubhouse."

The boys got the crate and carried it to a shady corner of the back yard. After a few hours of sawing, nailing, and painting, the clubhouse was finished. It was sure to be the setting for many fine adventures.

1. When and where does the story take place?
   - ○ **A.** at a neighbor's house in the winter
   - ○ **B.** at Arnie's house in the morning
   - ○ **C.** at Dustin's house in the fall
   - ○ **D.** at Ray's house in the summer

2. Who are the main characters in the story?
   - ○ **F.** Ray, Dustin, and Arnie
   - ○ **G.** Ray and Arnie
   - ○ **H.** Arnie and Dustin
   - ○ **J.** just Ray

3. Which of these story events takes place first?
   - ○ **A.** Delivery men arrive with the refrigerator.
   - ○ **B.** The boys look carefully at the backyard trees.
   - ○ **C.** Ray suggests that they make a tree house.
   - ○ **D.** The boys move the crate into the back yard.

4. What problem do the boys have?
   - ○ **F.** They must figure out how to build a clubhouse.
   - ○ **G.** They are not allowed to sleep in the yard overnight.
   - ○ **H.** There is not enough paint to decorate the clubhouse.
   - ○ **J.** Ray's mother will not let them use the back yard.

5. How do the boys resolve their problem?
   - ○ **A.** They find plenty of lumber to build a cabin.
   - ○ **B.** They make a clubhouse out of the refrigerator crate.
   - ○ **C.** Ray's mother helps them build the tree house.
   - ○ **D.** They decide to turn Ray's room into a clubhouse.

Name _____

Problem Solving and Decision Making

Read the passage and answer the questions that follow. Fill in the circle next to the best answer.

Kitten Trouble

The phone rang, but Ramón did not want to answer it. He knew it would be Carl with his daily emergency. "Hello," Ramón grumbled.

"Ramón, this isn't good," whined a gloomy, familiar voice. "It's about the kitten." It was Carl, of course. "Listen, Ramón. I must have been crazy to let you talk me into taking that kitten. I know it followed us home from school, but Mom says we can't keep it. We are now down to one goldfish — one terrified goldfish."

"Okay, Carl. Let's think about this. You know I can't take the kitten because we're all allergic to cats at my house. Do you know anyone who might want a new pet? What about your Aunt June?" Ramón asked.

"I don't know anyone. And Aunt June doesn't want a kitten. I've already asked." Carl fell silent, waiting for Ramón to come up with another suggestion.

"I've got an idea," said Ramón. "Stay there, I'll be right over." He found a shoe box and a roll of blue ribbon, and then he headed out the door.

At Carl's house, Ramón cut the ribbon and made a fluffy bow to tie around the kitten's neck. Then they put the kitten in the box without the top. The two boys walked down the block to the neighborhood grocery store. They stood outside the door, showing the kitten to everyone who came out.

Within minutes, Carl's neighbor Mrs. Solis said she would love to have the kitten. In fact, she said she had been thinking about going to the animal shelter to find a kitten that same day. She gave the boys a box of cookies to thank them.

As they walked home, Carl turned to Ramón. "When we work together, we really get results!"

Ramón just shook his head and kept walking.

1. What is the main problem in this story?
   - ◯ **A.** Ramón and his family are allergic to cats.
   - ◯ **B.** The boys need to find a new owner for the kitten.
   - ◯ **C.** Carl is always asking Ramón to solve his problems.
   - ◯ **D.** The kitten is catching and eating Carl's goldfish.

2. What decision did the boys make that led to this problem?
   - ◯ **F.** They decided to keep the kitten that followed them.
   - ◯ **G.** They decided that Ramón would not keep the kitten.
   - ◯ **H.** They decided to take the kitten to the animal shelter.
   - ◯ **J.** They decided to keep goldfish instead of the kitten.

3. Based on the way they solve their problem, what can you tell about the characters?
   - ◯ **A.** Ramón is serious, while Carl is fun-loving.
   - ◯ **B.** Ramón and Carl do not like one another very much.
   - ◯ **C.** Carl depends on Ramón to help him solve problems.
   - ◯ **D.** Both boys are excellent students.

4. How do the boys solve the problem?
   - ◯ **F.** They give the kitten to Mrs. Solis.
   - ◯ **G.** Carl leaves the kitten in a box at the grocery store.
   - ◯ **H.** They take the kitten to the animal shelter.
   - ◯ **J.** Ramón decides to keep the kitten himself.

5. Which of these is **not** a step in the boys' problem-solving process?
   - ◯ **A.** Ramón ties a ribbon around the kitten's neck.
   - ◯ **B.** The boys place the kitten in a box.
   - ◯ **C.** The boys show the kitten to grocery store customers.
   - ◯ **D.** Mrs. Solis gives the boys a box of cookies.

Name _____

Information and Study Skills

Read each question. Fill in the circle next to the best answer.

1. If you wanted to write a report on the life of George Washington, which reference source would you begin with?

    ○ **A.** monthly magazine
    ○ **B.** web site
    ○ **C.** primary source documents
    ○ **D.** encyclopedia

2. Where might you find a review of a movie you saw last year?

    ○ **F.** current newspapers
    ○ **G.** web site
    ○ **H.** trade book about making movies
    ○ **J.** encyclopedia

3. Which two sources would be most useful in finding information about candidates in an upcoming election?

    ○ **A.** current newspaper and web site
    ○ **B.** encyclopedia and magazine
    ○ **C.** interview with a candidate and encyclopedia
    ○ **D.** web site and trade book about elections

Read the passage and answer the questions that follow. Fill in the circle next to the best answer.

English scientist Isaac Newton had a sad childhood. After his father died, Isaac was raised by his grandmother. He was a lonely child, since he was not accepted by children in his grandmother's village. Young Newton spent most of his time reading and making things. As a result, when Newton entered Cambridge University, he knew more than most of his professors. Eventually, Newton's ideas about science changed the way people thought about the world around them.

4. What is this passage mainly about?
   - ○ **F.** Isaac Newton's early life
   - ○ **G.** Isaac Newton's father
   - ○ **H.** Isaac Newton's years at Cambridge
   - ○ **J.** Isaac Newton's ideas about science

5. Choose the best way to paraphrase the passage.
   - ○ **A.** Because Newton went to live with his grandmother, he was ignored by the other children in the village.
   - ○ **B.** Although Newton went to live with his grandmother as a boy, he did not have problems getting into Cambridge University.
   - ○ **C.** As a result of his lonely childhood, Newton spent time educating himself, and he went on to become an important scientist.
   - ○ **D.** Having a lonely childhood often leads to a successful career in science.

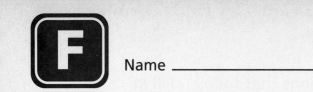

Name _____

VCV, VCCV, and VCCCV Patterns

Read each sentence. Fill in the circle next to the best answer.

1. Find the word that has the VCV pattern.
   - ○ **A.** hectic
   - ○ **B.** helpless
   - ○ **C.** history
   - ○ **D.** hesitant

2. Find the word that has the VCCV pattern.
   - ○ **F.** salad
   - ○ **G.** service
   - ○ **H.** simple
   - ○ **J.** settlement

Read each sentence. Choose the correct way to divide the underlined word into syllables. Fill in the circle next to the best answer.

3. The man carefully placed the <u>halter</u> on the horse.
   - ○ **A.** hal•ter
   - ○ **B.** ha•lter
   - ○ **C.** halt•er
   - ○ **D.** halte•r

4. Jan should decide what <u>amount</u> to spend.
   - ○ **F.** am•ount
   - ○ **G.** amo•unt
   - ○ **H.** a•mount
   - ○ **J.** amou•nt

5. My father collects <u>empty</u> boxes to use as storage.
   - ○ **A.** empt•y
   - ○ **B.** em•pt•y
   - ○ **C.** em•pty
   - ○ **D.** emp•ty

Name _____

Words Ending in *-ed* or *-ing*

Read each sentence, and find the base word for the underlined word. Fill in the circle next to the best answer.

1. Yesterday, John <u>tasted</u> broccoli for the very first time.
   ○ **A.** taste
   ○ **B.** tast
   ○ **C.** tas
   ○ **D.** tastes

2. I will be <u>humming</u> that tune all day.
   ○ **F.** humm
   ○ **G.** hums
   ○ **H.** hummin
   ○ **J.** hum

Read each sentence, and find the word that is made up of a base word and an ending. Fill in the circle next to the best answer.

3. Tad <u>inched</u> <u>toward</u> the hurt <u>bird</u> that lay by his <u>doorstep</u>.
   ○ **A.** toward
   ○ **B.** inched
   ○ **C.** bird
   ○ **D.** doorstep

4. <u>Since</u> Maria came <u>down</u> with a <u>cold</u>, she has been <u>sneezing</u> all day.
   ○ **F.** sneezing
   ○ **G.** Since
   ○ **H.** cold
   ○ **J.** down

5. The <u>woman</u> <u>investigated</u> the <u>dinosaur</u> bone <u>under</u> a microscope.
   ○ **A.** woman
   ○ **B.** dinosaur
   ○ **C.** investigated
   ○ **D.** under

Endings and Suffixes *-en, -ize, -ify*

Read each sentence. Then find the meaning of each underlined word. Fill in the circle next to the best answer.

1. Will this liquid <u>solidify</u> if we freeze it?
    - ○ **A.** the condition of being solid
    - ○ **B.** capable of being solid
    - ○ **C.** lack a solid state
    - ○ **D.** become solid

2. Let's try to <u>vaporize</u> the liquid over a burner.
    - ○ **F.** capable of being vapor
    - ○ **G.** lacking any vapor
    - ○ **H.** make into vapor
    - ○ **J.** full of vapors

3. You will <u>weaken</u> that plastic if you heat it.
    - ○ **A.** lacking weakness
    - ○ **B.** known to be weak
    - ○ **C.** capable of being weak
    - ○ **D.** cause to be weak

4. Some scientists can show us how to <u>beautify</u> our surroundings.
    - ○ **F.** make beautiful
    - ○ **G.** lacking beauty
    - ○ **H.** process of being beautiful
    - ○ **J.** in a beautiful way

5. The thought of studying science should not <u>frighten</u> any student.
    - ○ **A.** lack fright
    - ○ **B.** capable of having fright
    - ○ **C.** cause fright
    - ○ **D.** full of fright

Name _____

Prefixes *in-*, *im-*, and *con-*

Read each sentence. Then find the meaning of each underlined word. Fill in the circle next to the best answer.

1. Sometimes my older brother acts in an <u>immature</u> way.
   - ○ **A.** responsible
   - ○ **B.** friendly
   - ○ **C.** mean
   - ○ **D.** childish

2. I am <u>confident</u>, though, that he will do well in life.
   - ○ **F.** afraid
   - ○ **G.** sorry
   - ○ **H.** certain
   - ○ **J.** willing

3. It is <u>inaccurate</u> to say that I don't get along with my brother.
   - ○ **A.** meaningful
   - ○ **B.** not possible
   - ○ **C.** ridiculous
   - ○ **D.** not correct

4. I'm sure our <u>constant</u> arguing is only a bad habit.
   - ○ **F.** never ending
   - ○ **G.** pleasant
   - ○ **H.** senseless
   - ○ **J.** short-lived

5. In fact, my life would be <u>incomplete</u> without him.
   - ○ **A.** always the same
   - ○ **B.** boring
   - ○ **C.** not whole
   - ○ **D.** never dull

Name _____

Spelling

Find the correctly spelled word to complete each sentence. Fill in the circle beside your answer.

1. Alexis wants to be a _____ when she grows up.

   ○ **A.** laywer
   ○ **B.** lauwyer
   ○ **C.** lawyer
   ○ **D.** lauyer

2. She remembered to _____ plenty of study time in her schedule.

   ○ **F.** inclood
   ○ **G.** imclude
   ○ **H.** innclude
   ○ **J.** include

3. She was the only one who _____ all the questions correctly.

   ○ **A.** ansered
   ○ **B.** answerred
   ○ **C.** answerd
   ○ **D.** answered

4. Jonah volunteers at the hospital in his _____.

   ○ **F.** community
   ○ **G.** conmunity
   ○ **H.** cammunity
   ○ **J.** comunity

5. He tries hard to _____ his schoolwork with his time at the hospital.

   ○ **A.** ballance
   ○ **B.** balence
   ○ **C.** balance
   ○ **D.** belence

Go on

6. Kip thinks there is nothing like the _____ of the stage.

- ○ **F.** exsitement
- ○ **G.** excitemint
- ○ **H.** excitemunt
- ○ **J.** excitement

7. He is always _____ to plays on the radio.

- ○ **A.** listening
- ○ **B.** listenning
- ○ **C.** lissening
- ○ **D.** listeneing

8. The local theater group plans to _____ Kip in their summer show.

- ○ **F.** imvolve
- ○ **G.** innvolve
- ○ **H.** involve
- ○ **J.** envolve

9. Marnie has _____ had time to think of what she wants to be.

- ○ **A.** scarcelly
- ○ **B.** scarcly
- ○ **C.** scarceley
- ○ **D.** scarcely

10. She finds great _____ in almost everything she does.

- ○ **F.** amusement
- ○ **G.** amusment
- ○ **H.** amusemint
- ○ **J.** amusemeant

Vocabulary

Read each sentence. Fill in the circle next to the best answer.

1. Complete the sentence with the word that has a negative connotation.

   The little girl _____ an extra piece of cake.
   ○ **A.** bought   ○ **C.** demanded
   ○ **B.** requested   ○ **D.** ate

2. Complete the sentence with the word that has a neutral connotation.

   I was startled by the _____ noise of the birds.
   ○ **F.** deafening   ○ **H.** cheerful
   ○ **G.** screeching   ○ **J.** loud

3. Complete the sentence with the word that has a positive connotation.

   There is a _____ park right outside the city.
   ○ **A.** fantastic   ○ **C.** water
   ○ **B.** big   ○ **D.** strange

Read the dictionary entry. Then look at each sentence and decide the part of speech of the underlined word. Fill in the circle next to the best answer.

---
flush (flŭsh) *v.* **flushed, flush•ing, flush•es.** *—intr.* To turn red in the face. *—n.* A flow or rush of water. *—adj.* **flush•er, flush•est** Plentiful; overflowing.

---

4. The fields were <u>flush</u> with new wildflowers.
   ○ **F.** verb   ○ **H.** adjective
   ○ **G.** noun   ○ **J.** adverb

5. Carey <u>flushed</u> when the teacher announced his birthday.
   ○ **A.** verb   ○ **C.** adjective
   ○ **B.** noun   ○ **D.** adverb

Go on ⇨

Read the thesaurus entries. Then read each question and fill in the circle next to the best answer.

---

sad *adj.* Showing, expressing, or feeling unhappiness.
    melancholy Feeling a lingering sadness.
    sorrowful Experiencing a painful sadness, especially caused by loss.
    depressed Low in spirits.
    antonyms: glad, joyful

brave *adj.* Having or showing courage.
    fearless Having no fear; brave.
    bold Showing a tendency to seek out danger.
    valiant Possessing valor; brave in a heroic way.
    antonyms: cowardly, fearful

---

6. Which word best replaces the underlined word in the following sentence?

    Tina's <u>sad</u> mood continued for weeks after her best friend moved away.

    ○ **F.** joyful
    ○ **G.** valiant
    ○ **H.** fearful
    ○ **J.** melancholy

7. Which word means the **opposite** of the underlined word in the following sentence?

    The <u>brave</u> firefighters continually risked their lives to help others.

    ○ **A.** depressed
    ○ **B.** cowardly
    ○ **C.** glad
    ○ **D.** fearless

Read the dictionary entry. Then choose the form of the word that best completes each sentence. Fill in the circle next to the best answer.

cruise (kr$\overline{oo}$z) *v.* **cruised, cruis•ing, cruis•es.** To sail or travel in an unhurried way.

8. A police car _____ the streets of the city last night.
   - ○ **F.** cruises
   - ○ **G.** cruising
   - ○ **H.** cruised
   - ○ **J.** cruise

9. Every day, taxi drivers will _____ the empty streets looking for fares.
   - ○ **A.** cruised
   - ○ **B.** cruising
   - ○ **C.** cruises
   - ○ **D.** cruise

10. Daniel admires the coastline while he is _____ in his brother's new boat.
    - ○ **F.** cruise
    - ○ **G.** cruising
    - ○ **H.** cruises
    - ○ **J.** cruised

Name _____

Grammar

Read each sentence. Fill in the circle next to the best answer.

1. Complete the sentence with a verb that agrees with the subject.

   John and the others _____ trying out for a part in the play.
   - ○ **A.** is
   - ○ **B.** was
   - ○ **C.** are
   - ○ **D.** be

2. Complete the sentence with a verb in the past tense.

   They _____ their lines together last week.
   - ○ **F.** practice
   - ○ **G.** practices
   - ○ **H.** will practice
   - ○ **J.** practiced

3. Complete the sentence with a regular verb in the past tense.

   Sue _____ through her part two or three times a day.
   - ○ **A.** thought
   - ○ **B.** ran
   - ○ **C.** went
   - ○ **D.** walked

4. Complete the sentence with a verb in the present perfect tense.

   All the friends _____ together to learn their parts.
   - ○ **F.** have worked
   - ○ **G.** had worked
   - ○ **H.** will work
   - ○ **J.** worked

5. Complete the sentence with a verb in the future tense.

   Each student _____ for a different part in the play.
   - ○ **A.** had auditioned
   - ○ **B.** auditions
   - ○ **C.** will audition
   - ○ **D.** auditioned

6. Complete the sentence with the correct verb in the past tense.

John _____ Silvia how to make her voice reach the back of the theater.

○ **F.** learned   ○ **H.** teach
○ **G.** learn   ○ **J.** taught

7. Complete the sentence with the correct verb in the present tense.

"Please _____ the script on the table while you practice," John said.

○ **A.** lay   ○ **C.** lie
○ **B.** laid   ○ **D.** have laid

8. Complete the sentence with the correct verb in the present tense.

Matt _____ Joe his copy of the script.

○ **F.** borrows
○ **G.** borrowed
○ **H.** lend
○ **J.** lends

9. Complete the sentence with a verb in the past perfect tense.

Tran _____ this play at his old school.

○ **A.** has performed
○ **B.** have performed
○ **C.** will perform
○ **D.** had performed

10. Complete the sentence with a verb in the future tense.

The play _____ to great reviews if everyone does his or her best.

○ **F.** has opened
○ **G.** had opened
○ **H.** will open
○ **J.** have opened

Name _____

Writing Skills

Read each numbered sentence or incomplete sentence. Then find the best way to correct each one. Fill in the circle next to your answer.

1. Tanya was going to visit her cousin Eric he lives in Parkville.
   - ○ **A.** Tanya was going to visit her cousin. Eric he lives in Parkville.
   - ○ **B.** Tanya was going to visit. Her cousin Eric he lives in Parkville.
   - ○ **C.** Tanya was going to visit her cousin Eric, he lives in Parkville.
   - ○ **D.** Tanya was going to visit her cousin Eric. He lives in Parkville.

2. Eric and Tanya and the other family members.
   - ○ **F.** Eric and Tanya; and the other family members.
   - ○ **G.** Eric and Tanya. And the other family members went to the zoo.
   - ○ **H.** Eric and Tanya and the other family members went to the zoo.
   - ○ **J.** Eric and Tanya and the other family members. Went to the zoo.

Complete each sentence with the most exact noun or verb. Fill in the circle next to the best answer.

3. The baby foxes _____ toward their mother.
    - ○ **A.** walked
    - ○ **B.** ran
    - ○ **C.** moved
    - ○ **D.** tumbled

4. Karin's new puppy _____ a bowlful of food.
    - ○ **F.** gobbled
    - ○ **G.** ate
    - ○ **H.** chewed
    - ○ **J.** had

5. We heard loud _____ as we neared the birdhouse.
    - ○ **A.** yelling
    - ○ **B.** noises
    - ○ **C.** squawking
    - ○ **D.** crying

Discovering Ancient Cultures

Level 6, Theme 4

Theme Skills Test Record

Student _____ Date _____

Student Record Form

	Possible Score	Criterion Score	Student Score
Part A: Author's Viewpoint: Bias and Assumption	5	4	
Part B: Cause and Effect	5	4	
Part C: Topic, Main Idea, and Details	5	4	
Part D: Information and Study Skills	5	4	
Part E: Suffixes -ic, -al, and -ure	5	4	
Part F: Suffixes -ion and -ation	5	4	
Part G: Unstressed Syllables	5	4	
Part H: Spelling	10	8	
Part I: Vocabulary	10	8	
Part J: Grammar	10	8	
Part K: Writing Skills	5	4	
TOTAL	70	56	
Total Student Score x 1.43 =			%

Name _____

Author's Viewpoint: Bias and Assumption

Read the passage and answer the questions that follow. Fill in the circle next to the best answer.

The Incas of Ancient Peru

The Incas were one of the greatest ancient civilizations. Their South American empire lasted for over 400 years. It probably would have lasted for thousands of years if the Spanish had not interfered. The Incas' beautiful capital city, in present-day Peru, had grand temples made of gold and stone. In total, the empire stretched for over 2,000 miles along South America's western coast. It was home to between six and eight million people.

Remarkable engineering was one characteristic that made the Incas great. They built strong suspension bridges across deep valleys. Their buildings were made of stone blocks that fit together neatly without mortar. The fit of the blocks was so perfect that a knife blade could not be slipped between them. The Incas also built canals to carry water from rivers and streams to their fields.

Skilled craftspeople made beautiful jewelry from metals and precious stones. Other workers made fine ceramic pottery and woven fabrics. Some examples of these products still exist today. However, greedy fortune hunters found and sold much of what remained.

The Incas developed many useful sciences. Astronomers drew charts of the solar system. They helped farmers know when to plant and harvest crops. Healers used herbs and other plants to create a variety of medicines. In fact, the use of quinine to treat malaria is thought to have come from the Incas.

This marvelous empire came to an end after being discovered by Spanish explorers. In 1532 Francisco Pizarro and his soldiers were welcomed warmly by the Incas. In return for the Incas' kindness, Pizarro kidnapped the Inca emperor and eventually killed him. The Spaniards took control of the empire and forced the Incas to work for them in gold and silver mines. By 1571, the great Inca empire had fallen into ruin.

Go on

---

1. What is the author's viewpoint in the passage?
   - ○ **A.** The Incas were a marvelous and advanced civilization.
   - ○ **B.** The Incas were mainly important because of their science.
   - ○ **C.** The Incas should have been able to overcome the Spanish army.
   - ○ **D.** The Incas ruled for too short a time to be a really great empire.

2. Which of these is an assumption rather than a fact?
   - ○ **F.** The Inca's South American empire lasted for over 400 years.
   - ○ **G.** It probably would have lasted for thousands of years if the Spanish had not interfered.
   - ○ **H.** The empire stretched for over 2,000 miles along South America's western coast.
   - ○ **J.** It was home to between six and eight million people.

3. Which words in the second paragraph help you identify the author's bias?
   - ○ **A.** engineering, buildings
   - ○ **B.** suspension, canals
   - ○ **C.** strong, stone
   - ○ **D.** remarkable, perfect

4. Which of these best describes the author's viewpoint about fortune hunters?
   - ○ **F.** positive
   - ○ **G.** negative
   - ○ **H.** unbiased
   - ○ **J.** neutral

5. Which of the following sentences is free of author's bias?
   - ○ **A.** The Incas' beautiful capital city, in present-day Peru, had grand temples made of gold and stone.
   - ○ **B.** This marvelous empire came to an end after being discovered by Spanish explorers.
   - ○ **C.** The Incas also built canals to carry water from rivers and streams to their fields.
   - ○ **D.** In return for the Incas' kindness, Pizarro kidnapped the Inca emperor and eventually killed him.

STOP

Name _____

Cause and Effect

Read the passage and answer the questions that follow. Fill in the circle next to the best answer.

The Mighty Nile

The ancient Egyptian empire began about 5,000 years ago and lasted for about 3,000 years. No one is sure exactly where the Egyptian people came from. One group of people settled around the mouth of the Nile River, or the Nile Delta. Another group settled in the Nile Valley. To this day, the Nile is an important part of life in Egypt.

Early Egyptians considered the Nile to be sacred. In a desert country such as Egypt, the Nile's waters made a civilized way of life possible. The river provided a water highway for getting from one place to another. More important, though, was the role of the Nile in agriculture.

Each year in the spring, heavy rains would fall over central Africa where the Nile began. Snows would begin to melt on nearby mountain-tops. As the rain and snowmelt flowed into the Nile, the river would flood its banks. When the flood waters subsided, they left behind a layer of rich, fertile soil.

The early Egyptians came to expect and even celebrate these annual floods. After the flood, the people would plant crops to provide food for the coming year. Since food and water were plentiful, people had time for other activities. For example, they developed a system of writing. They also built monuments and structures that remain to this day, such as the great pyramids at Giza.

Modern Egyptians still live mainly along the narrow strip of fertile land on either side of the Nile. The Nile no longer floods annually. In 1970, a dam was completed that forms a very large lake. Waters from this lake are used to irrigate crops on a regular schedule. Even though the flow of the river beneath the dam has been reduced, the Nile remains important to the people of Egypt.

1. Why did ancient people settle near the Nile River?
   - ○ **A.** They were tired of moving from place to place.
   - ○ **B.** They could not cross the river to move deeper into the desert.
   - ○ **C.** The river's water made a civilized way of life possible.
   - ○ **D.** The nearby desert provided access to food and camels.

2. Why did the Egyptians think of the Nile as sacred?
   - ○ **F.** It was good for boating.
   - ○ **G.** It was near the pyramids.
   - ○ **H.** It flooded each year in the spring.
   - ○ **J.** It gave them what they needed for life.

3. What caused the Nile to flood in the spring?
   - ○ **A.** flood gates opening in the dam
   - ○ **B.** rain and melting snow
   - ○ **C.** strong ocean tides
   - ○ **D.** overflowing irrigation canals

4. Why were the early Egyptians able to build monuments?
   - ○ **F.** They did not have to work hard to get food and water.
   - ○ **G.** They had plenty of building materials at hand.
   - ○ **H.** They were skilled craftspeople with years of experience.
   - ○ **J.** They had learned the process while building a dam.

5. Why is flooding no longer an annual event on the Nile?
   - ○ **A.** The desert has spread into areas where the river once flowed.
   - ○ **B.** The ancient Egyptians used most of the water in the river.
   - ○ **C.** People have built too many irrigation canals and there is not enough water.
   - ○ **D.** A dam was built to control the flow of the water.

Topic, Main Idea, and Details

Read the passage and answer the questions that follow. Fill in the circle next to the best answer.

The City of Tikal

For about one thousand years, Tikal was the grandest city of the Maya people. It was the center of life for this ancient civilization until about A.D. 900. Tikal was built deep in the jungles of present-day Guatemala. Its magnificent buildings housed activities such as painting, writing, sculpture, and astronomy.

Tikal was built around a large central plaza. This is where most religious ceremonies and other public events took place. It was also the location for the public market, where a great variety of goods were sold or traded. The Great Plaza was bordered by pyramids with heights of 200 feet or more. These stone pyramids were built in the shape of terraced steps leading up to a flat roof. Small temples sat on top of each pyramid's roof.

Around the Great Plaza were the homes of Tikal's ruling class. These homes were very luxurious and could be as many as three stories high. Between the long stone buildings, stairways and passages overlooked comfortable courtyards. The interior walls of the houses were plastered and painted. There is even evidence that the wealthy residents had curtains for the windows and animal skins for the floors.

Fanning out from the Great Plaza were wide walkways. These walkways were plastered and bordered with walls. They led to additional civic buildings and pyramids in and around the city. At the end of one walkway was the largest known Maya pyramid. Towering 212 feet above the jungle floor, it is often described as a mountain of stone.

For some mysterious reason, Tikal and the other great Maya cities were deserted suddenly. Residents apparently moved back into the jungle or out to farmlands. Without workers to maintain it, Tikal was quickly overgrown by jungle plants. It remained hidden from view until it was rediscovered by European scientists in the nineteenth century.

Go on ⇨

1. What is this passage mainly about?
   - ○ **A.** Tikal
   - ○ **B.** Maya people
   - ○ **C.** pyramids
   - ○ **D.** lost cities

2. What is the topic of the second paragraph?
   - ○ **F.** religious ceremonies
   - ○ **G.** the public market
   - ○ **H.** the Great Plaza
   - ○ **J.** pyramid shapes

3. What main idea does the following detail support?

   The interior walls of the houses were plastered and painted.
   - ○ **A.** The homes had curtains for the windows and animal skins for the floors.
   - ○ **B.** Homes of the ruling class were comfortable and luxurious.
   - ○ **C.** The homes, some with several stories, were long stone buildings.
   - ○ **D.** Wide walkways fanned out from the central plaza.

4. What is the topic of the fourth paragraph?
   - ○ **F.** other pyramids around the city
   - ○ **G.** civic buildings
   - ○ **H.** the largest Maya pyramid
   - ○ **J.** the wide walkways

5. Which detail best supports the main idea that Tikal was the grandest city of the Maya people?
   - ○ **A.** It was built deep in the jungle of present-day Guatemala.
   - ○ **B.** Its magnificent buildings housed activities such as painting, writing, sculpture, and astronomy.
   - ○ **C.** Most religious ceremonies and other public events took place in the Great Plaza.
   - ○ **D.** For some mysterious reason, Tikal and other great Maya cities were deserted suddenly.

Name _____

Information and Study Skills

Read each passage. The first passage is from a nonfiction book about the Anasazi and the second is from a brochure about Mesa Verde National Park. Then answer the questions that follow. Fill in the circle next to the best answer.

Passage 1

For many years, the Anasazi lived in great stone cities carved into the edge of Mesa Verde's cliffs. The cliff dwellings looked out over deep canyons. It isn't clear why the Anasazi chose to live in this unlikely setting. It may have been to protect them from bad weather or enemies. Whatever the reason, the cliff dwellings remain today as a source of mystery and beauty.

The cliff dwellings were built in the 1200s by the Anasazi. They ranged in size from one-room houses to huge villages containing hundreds of rooms. The interior of the rooms varied in quality. Some walls were left as rough, blank stone. Other rooms were plastered inside. Often, decorative scenes were painted on the walls.

Less than a hundred years after the Anasazi built their cliff houses, they disappeared. No one knows why they left or where they moved to. However, clues to the Anasazi way of life can still be found in the cliffs of Mesa Verde.

Passage 2

Mesa Verde National Park preserves the remains of a thousand-year-old culture. The people who lived here are called the Anasazi, from a Navajo word meaning "ancient ones." These people left no written record. However, the ruins tell the story of a people skilled in building, basket making, and pottery. We can also tell that they cleared land on the mesa tops and raised a few crops.

The Anasazi appear to have been an advanced society. They passed what they knew from one generation to the next. The people who lived in the cliff dwellings inherited a thriving civilization. They kept and built upon important earlier achievements in community living and in the arts.

Go on

1. If you were taking notes from the first passage, which of these might be a good heading for a note card?
   - ○ **A.** Decorative Drawings
   - ○ **B.** Mesa Verde
   - ○ **C.** Anasazi Ceremonies
   - ○ **D.** Anasazi Cliff Dwellings

2. Which detail is important enough to include on a note card about the first paragraph?
   - ○ **F.** canyons were deep
   - ○ **G.** unclear where they lived
   - ○ **H.** dwellings built to protect
   - ○ **J.** dwellings were beautiful

3. If you were taking notes from the second passage, what might be a good heading for a note card?
   - ○ **A.** Mesa Verde National Park
   - ○ **B.** Farming on the Mesa
   - ○ **C.** A Thriving Civilization
   - ○ **D.** The Anasazi People

4. Which detail would you leave out of a note card about the second passage?
   - ○ **F.** ruins tell a story
   - ○ **G.** left no written record
   - ○ **H.** Anasazi means "ancient ones"
   - ○ **J.** people skilled in building and basket making

5. What information other than the topic and details should be included on a note card?
   - ○ **A.** a list of all topics and subtopics covered by the source
   - ○ **B.** the titles and page numbers of sources used
   - ○ **C.** an exact copy of each sentence you plan to use
   - ○ **D.** all direct quotes found in the source material

Name _____

Suffixes *-ic, -al,* and *-ure*

Read each sentence, and find the base word for the underlined word. Fill in the circle next to the best answer.

1. We love to watch the <u>comical</u> behavior of the baby kittens.
   - ○ **A.** come
   - ○ **B.** comedy
   - ○ **C.** comic
   - ○ **D.** commercial

2. The charity gained <u>exposure</u> from the news article about its 5K race.
   - ○ **F.** expose
   - ○ **G.** sure
   - ○ **H.** pose
   - ○ **J.** explain

3. The store's new <u>economic</u> policy allowed it to cut costs and save money.
   - ○ **A.** nominate
   - ○ **B.** ecology
   - ○ **C.** continue
   - ○ **D.** economy

Read each sentence. Then find the meaning of the underlined word. Fill in the circle next to the best answer.

4. Everyone looked into the <u>tidal</u> pool to watch the starfish.
   - ○ **F.** having to do with water
   - ○ **G.** relating to the tide
   - ○ **H.** relating to starfish
   - ○ **J.** having to do with science

5. The rancher kept the younger calves in an <u>enclosure</u> near the farmhouse.
   - ○ **A.** grassy pasture
   - ○ **B.** large barn
   - ○ **C.** close position
   - ○ **D.** closed-in space

Suffixes *-ion* and *-ation*

Read each sentence, and find the base word for the underlined word. Fill in the circle next to the best answer.

1. The students paid close <u>attention</u> to their teacher.
   - ○ **A.** tension
   - ○ **B.** attend
   - ○ **C.** tendency
   - ○ **D.** attitude

2. Everyone helped with <u>preparations</u> for the art show.
   - ○ **F.** repair
   - ○ **G.** parade
   - ○ **H.** prepare
   - ○ **J.** predict

3. She chose her answer by process of <u>elimination</u>.
   - ○ **A.** limit
   - ○ **B.** imagine
   - ○ **C.** eliminate
   - ○ **D.** element

Read each sentence. Then find the meaning of the underlined word. Fill in the circle next to the best answer.

4. Trevor made a very polite <u>introduction</u>.
   - ○ **F.** without introducing
   - ○ **G.** place for introducing
   - ○ **H.** one who introduces
   - ○ **J.** process of introducing

5. The pianist was an <u>inspiration</u> to all who heard her play.
   - ○ **A.** one who inspires
   - ○ **B.** process of inspiring
   - ○ **C.** without inspiring
   - ○ **D.** inclined to inspire

Unstressed Syllables

Read each sentence. Then choose the word in which the syllables are stressed correctly. Fill in the circle next to the best answer.

1. The polluted river waters will soon <u>contaminate</u> the ocean.
   - ○ **A.** CON•tam•i•nate
   - ○ **B.** con•tam•I•nate
   - ○ **C.** con•tam•i•NATE
   - ○ **D.** con•TAM•i•nate

2. Jorge waited impatiently to cross the busy <u>intersection</u>.
   - ○ **F.** in•TER•sec•tion
   - ○ **G.** in•ter•sec•TION
   - ○ **H.** in•ter•SEC•tion
   - ○ **J.** IN•ter•sec•tion

3. I <u>generally</u> enjoy going to the movies, but today I'd rather stay home and read.
   - ○ **A.** gen•er•AL•ly
   - ○ **B.** GEN•er•al•ly
   - ○ **C.** gen•er•al•LY
   - ○ **D.** gen•ER•al•ly

4. Dawn can be very <u>insensitive</u> when she teases her younger brother.
   - ○ **F.** in•SEN•si•tive
   - ○ **G.** in•sen•SI•tive
   - ○ **H.** IN•sen•si•tive
   - ○ **J.** in•sen•si•TIVE

5. The high <u>precipitation</u> levels in our county caused the rivers to flood.
   - ○ **A.** pre•CIP•i•ta•tion
   - ○ **B.** pre•cip•i•ta•TION
   - ○ **C.** PRE•cip•i•ta•tion
   - ○ **D.** pre•cip•i•TA•tion

Name _____

Spelling

Find the correctly spelled word to complete each sentence.
Fill in the circle beside your answer.

1. Some people study _____ cultures and then teach others what they learn.
   - ○ **A.** anshent
   - ○ **B.** anshient
   - ○ **C.** ancient
   - ○ **D.** antient

2. They point out each _____ between people who lived long ago and those who live today.
   - ○ **F.** connecteion
   - ○ **G.** connecshun
   - ○ **H.** connecsion
   - ○ **J.** connection

3. Some people travel to other countries to _____ ties with a culture.
   - ○ **A.** establish
   - ○ **B.** establesh
   - ○ **C.** establich
   - ○ **D.** istablish

4. Their _____ is to learn all they can about the land and its people.
   - ○ **F.** mition
   - ○ **G.** micion
   - ○ **H.** mission
   - ○ **J.** mishon

5. Sometimes they find evidence of very old _____.
   - ○ **A.** construcsion
   - ○ **B.** construction
   - ○ **C.** construcshun
   - ○ **D.** construcion

Go on ⟶

6. It takes a lot of _____ strength to dig for ruins.

   ○ **F.** physacul
   ○ **G.** physacal
   ○ **H.** physicul
   ○ **J.** physical

7. It is _____ to find unbroken artifacts.

   ○ **A.** difficult
   ○ **B.** difficalt
   ○ **C.** diffucult
   ○ **D.** diffacult

8. Most digs require careful _____ by those involved.

   ○ **F.** cooperateion
   ○ **G.** cooperashun
   ○ **H.** cooperation
   ○ **J.** cooperacion

9. The workers have great _____ for these older cultures.

   ○ **A.** admeration
   ○ **B.** admiracion
   ○ **C.** admeracion
   ○ **D.** admiration

10. Even the smallest piece of broken pottery can be an important _____ of life in another time.

   ○ **F.** exampel
   ○ **G.** example
   ○ **H.** exsample
   ○ **J.** exampil

Name _____

Vocabulary

Read each sentence. Then find the word that means nearly the same as the underlined word. Fill in the circle next to the best answer.

1. The scientists spent weeks trying to figure out the <u>complicated</u> writing system.
   - ○ **A.** interesting
   - ○ **B.** intricate
   - ○ **C.** dull
   - ○ **D.** simple

2. With magnifying lenses, they <u>examined</u> each and every symbol.
   - ○ **F.** copied
   - ○ **G.** expressed
   - ○ **H.** wrote
   - ○ **J.** inspected

3. The symbols were drawn in a circular <u>style</u> unlike any they had seen before.
   - ○ **A.** tone
   - ○ **B.** manner
   - ○ **C.** color
   - ○ **D.** time

4. The youngest scientist tried to <u>persuade</u> the others to keep working even when they were ready to quit.
   - ○ **F.** convince
   - ○ **G.** understand
   - ○ **H.** permit
   - ○ **J.** allow

Read the sentence. Then find the meaning of each underlined word. Fill in the circle next to the best answer.

5. The dusty trunks were <u>bound</u> with strong ropes.
   - ○ **A.** limited
   - ○ **B.** leaped
   - ○ **C.** tied
   - ○ **D.** headed

6. "What do the markings <u>mean</u>?" the man asked.
   - ○ **F.** tell
   - ○ **G.** average
   - ○ **H.** unkind
   - ○ **J.** slight

Theme Skills Tests, Level 6   Theme 4: Discovering Ancient Cultures   **85**

7. The explorer began to <u>pound</u> a hammer against the lock.
- ○ **A.** measure of weight
- ○ **B.** strike firmly
- ○ **C.** throb
- ○ **D.** shelter for animals

Look at the chart below. Then read each sentence, and find the meaning of the underlined word. Fill in the circle next to the best answer.

Prefixes	Meanings
ad- re-	toward or to again or back

Suffixes	Meanings
-ant, -or -ful	a person who does full of

8. It often takes a while for people to <u>adapt</u> when they travel to foreign lands.
- ○ **F.** move away from
- ○ **G.** fight back
- ○ **H.** agree with
- ○ **J.** get used to

9. <u>Assistants</u> from many countries are hired for each new dig.
- ○ **A.** relating to assisting
- ○ **B.** able to assist
- ○ **C.** people who assist
- ○ **D.** the process of assisting

10. Often, a <u>translator</u> is needed to make sure everything goes smoothly.
- ○ **F.** able to translate
- ○ **G.** one who translates
- ○ **H.** relating to translating
- ○ **J.** full of translating

Name _____

Grammar

Complete each sentence with the correct adjective. Fill in the circle next to the best answer.

1. _____ pot that I am holding could be thousands of years old.
   - ○ **A.** This
   - ○ **B.** Those
   - ○ **C.** That
   - ○ **D.** These

2. Have you ever seen _____ item like this one?
   - ○ **F.** those
   - ○ **G.** these
   - ○ **H.** a
   - ○ **J.** an

3. I think the clay comes from _____ mountains over there.
   - ○ **A.** this
   - ○ **B.** these
   - ○ **C.** that
   - ○ **D.** those

4. Did you know that _____ bowl you found is priceless?
   - ○ **F.** the Roman
   - ○ **G.** The Roman
   - ○ **H.** The roman
   - ○ **J.** the roman

Complete each sentence with the correct adjective form. Fill in the circle next to the best answer.

5. This is the _____ of the two vases.
   - ○ **A.** more valuable
   - ○ **B.** valuabler
   - ○ **C.** most valuable
   - ○ **D.** valuablest

6. Only the very _____ people were able to afford gold jewelry.

- ○ **F.** richer
- ○ **G.** more rich
- ○ **H.** richest
- ○ **J.** most rich

7. Which of these two necklaces shows the _____ quality of work?

- ○ **A.** goodest
- ○ **B.** better
- ○ **C.** more good
- ○ **D.** best

Complete each sentence with the correct adverb form. Fill in the circle next to the best answer.

8. We have worked _____ at this site than at the last one.

- ○ **F.** carefuller
- ○ **G.** carefullest
- ○ **H.** more carefully
- ○ **J.** most carefully

9. It is impossible to say which person in the group has worked _____.

- ○ **A.** hardest
- ○ **B.** harder
- ○ **C.** more hard
- ○ **D.** most hard

10. Of all the groups here, ours has worked _____.

- ○ **F.** more quicker
- ○ **G.** more quickly
- ○ **H.** most quickest
- ○ **J.** most quickly

Writing Skills

Name _____

Read each numbered sentence. Then choose the sentence in which adjectives make it more descriptive and interesting. Fill in the circle next to the best answer.

1. Years ago, people lived in caves.
   - ○ **A.** Years ago, when ice covered much of the planet, people lived in caves.
   - ○ **B.** Years ago, people lived comfortably in caves.
   - ○ **C.** Years and years ago, people lived and worked in caves.
   - ○ **D.** Many years ago, some people lived in dry, comfortable caves.

2. Mammoths and tigers roamed the land.
   - ○ **F.** During that time, mammoths and tigers roamed the land.
   - ○ **G.** Mammoths and tigers roamed freely throughout the land.
   - ○ **H.** Wooly mammoths and saber-toothed tigers roamed the forested land.
   - ○ **J.** Mammoths, as well as tigers, roamed freely throughout the land.

3. The landscape was covered with trees and surrounded by mountains.
   - ○ **A.** It is true that the landscape was covered with trees and surrounded by mountains.
   - ○ **B.** The landscape, which was covered with trees, was surrounded by mountains.
   - ○ **C.** Surrounded by mountains, the landscape was covered by trees and other plants.
   - ○ **D.** The prehistoric landscape was covered with unusual trees and surrounded by steep mountains.

4. Game provided meals for the cave people.

    ○ **F.** Plentiful game provided hearty meals for the cave people.

    ○ **G.** Sometimes game provided meals for the cave people.

    ○ **H.** Game provided plenty of food and sport for the cave people.

    ○ **J.** There was plenty of game, and it provided meals for the cave people.

5. Footpaths wound into the forest.

    ○ **A.** Footpaths wound into the forest in all directions.

    ○ **B.** The bumpy footpaths wound into the lush forest.

    ○ **C.** Deep into the forest, footpaths wound crazily.

    ○ **D.** Footpaths wound throughout the forest's trees and plants.

Doers and Dreamers

Level 6, Theme 5

Theme Skills Test Record

Student _____ Date _____

Student Record Form		Possible Score	Criterion Score	Student Score
Part A:	Propaganda	5	4	
Part B:	Problem Solving	5	4	
Part C:	Compare and Contrast	5	4	
Part D:	Information and Study Skills	5	4	
Part E:	Word Parts *ven* and *graph*	5	4	
Part F:	Plurals	5	4	
Part G:	Suffixes *-ent/-ence, -ant/-ance, -able/-ible, -ate*	5	4	
Part H:	Spelling	10	8	
Part I:	Vocabulary	10	8	
Part J:	Grammar	10	8	
Part K:	Writing Skills	5	4	
TOTAL		70	56	
		Total Student Score x 1.43 =		%

Name _____

Propaganda

Read the advertisement and answer the questions that follow. Fill in the circle next to the best answer.

Buy a Biggie Wheel!

Have you been looking for the perfect bicycle? Look no further, because Biggie Wheel bicycles are made well and priced right. Here are just a few good reasons why you should make your next bike a Biggie Wheel.

Everyone who rides a Biggie Wheel loves it. You, too, will wonder how you ever rode another brand of bike. Biggie Wheel's specially designed seat and supersized tires make the ride smooth and comfortable.

Biggie Wheel riders win the race. Our lightweight titanium gears give you that competitive edge. You will feel like a champion as you cross the finish line on your Biggie Wheel.

Long-distance riders will appreciate Biggie Wheel's low-maintenance features. Here is what famous long-distance rider Jan Delbar had to say: "I've ridden my Biggie Wheel for many long miles. I've never had to stop during a trip to make pesky repairs. These bikes hold up, even under harsh conditions."

If you still need a reason to buy a Biggie Wheel bike this week, hang on tight. For a limited time, we will give you a trade-in on your old bike when you buy a new Biggie Wheel. Shop soon at your neighborhood Biggie Wheel dealer to take advantage of this special offer. All your friends and neighbors will be buying their new Biggie Wheel bikes, too!

1. What is the purpose of the advertisement?
   - ○ **A.** to get more people to ride bicycles
   - ○ **B.** to get people to buy Biggie Wheel bicycles
   - ○ **C.** to get people to enter competitive bike races
   - ○ **D.** to get people to support Jan Delbar

2. Which statement is an overgeneralization?
   - ○ **F.** Everyone who rides a Biggie Wheel loves it.
   - ○ **G.** Have you been looking for the perfect bicycle?
   - ○ **H.** Biggie Wheel riders win the race.
   - ○ **J.** These bikes hold up, even under harsh conditions.

3. Which propaganda technique is used in the following sentence?

   You will feel like a champion as you cross the finish line on your Biggie Wheel.
   - ○ **A.** transfer
   - ○ **B.** overgeneralization
   - ○ **C.** faulty cause-and-effect
   - ○ **D.** testimonial

4. Which propaganda technique is used in the following sentences?

   Here is what famous long-distance rider Jan Delbar had to say: "I've ridden my Biggie Wheel for many long miles. I've never had to stop during a trip to make pesky repairs. These bikes hold up under harsh conditions."
   - ○ **F.** overgeneralization
   - ○ **G.** faulty cause-and-effect
   - ○ **H.** testimonial
   - ○ **J.** bandwagon

5. Which of the following sentences is an example of bandwagon?
   - ○ **A.** Look no further because Biggie Wheel bikes are made well and priced right.
   - ○ **B.** You, too, will wonder how you ever rode another brand of bike.
   - ○ **C.** Our lightweight titanium gears give you that competitive edge.
   - ○ **D.** All your friends and neighbors will be buying their new Biggie Wheel bikes, too!

STOP

Problem Solving

Read the story and answer the questions that follow. Fill in the circle next to the best answer.

New in Town

When I first met Cassandra, she had just moved to Canyon Creek. She was nice enough, but she didn't make much of an effort. My friends and I asked her to sit with us at lunch that first day, and she smiled and said, "Oh, no. I don't want to bother you." We tried again the next day and got the same answer, so we quit trying.

The next week Mrs. Johnson asked Cassandra if she'd like to join the girls' basketball team. "Oh, no," she said. "I don't play very well." Mrs. Johnson assured her that none of us played very well and that we could all improve together. Cassandra still told her no. Well, Mrs. Johnson believes that we should all have an activity, so she just kept naming clubs and teams until she found one for Cassandra. She went through a long list until finally Cassandra gave in. "Soccer," she blurted out. "I'll play soccer."

Cassandra lasted on the soccer team for exactly half of one practice. When she kept running in the wrong direction, Coach asked her if she had ever played before. "No," she said. She looked like she was about to cry.

Coach tried to shoo the rest of the team away so she could talk to Cassandra, but nobody moved. "Why did you want to join the soccer team if you've never played?" Coach asked.

"I don't know," Cassandra admitted. "It just popped out of my mouth. I'm sorry I ever said I would play."

That's when my friend, Ann Marie, stepped in. She asked Cassandra what she liked to do when she wasn't at school. Cassandra surprised everybody when she said she liked to play the flute. Ann Marie smiled and said, "Well, why don't you join the band? We need all the help we can get." And for the first time in two weeks, Cassandra smiled. Really smiled.

Go on

"That would be great," she said. "I guess I was too nervous about being the new kid. I thought nobody would like me. Thanks for the suggestion, Ann Marie." From then on, Cassandra sat with us every day at lunch. She's one of my best friends, and she's the best flute player in the band.

1. At the beginning of the passage, what problem does Cassandra have?
   ○ **A.** She's just moved to town and is nervous.
   ○ **B.** She doesn't know where to sit at lunch.
   ○ **C.** She forgets how to play basketball.
   ○ **D.** She doesn't want to play the flute.

2. Which of these is **not** a possible solution to Cassandra's problem?
   ○ **F.** to join the basketball team
   ○ **G.** to sit with the others at lunch
   ○ **H.** to join the soccer team
   ○ **J.** to move to a new town

3. How does Cassandra make her problem worse?
   ○ **A.** She tries hard to make new friends.
   ○ **B.** She says "no" too many times.
   ○ **C.** She joins the basketball team.
   ○ **D.** She learns to play soccer.

4. How does Cassandra finally solve her problem?
   ○ **F.** She learns to play the flute.
   ○ **G.** She makes friends away from school.
   ○ **H.** She finds the right activity for her.
   ○ **J.** She decides to stay on the soccer team.

5. How could Cassandra have solved her problem earlier?
   ○ **A.** by sitting alone in the lunchroom
   ○ **B.** by accepting invitations and being herself
   ○ **C.** by learning the rules of soccer before practice
   ○ **D.** by telling Mrs. Johnson she didn't want to join anything

Compare and Contrast

Read the passage and answer the questions that follow. Fill in the circle next to the best answer.

Artists at Work

Henri Matisse and Marc Chagall were both famous artists. The two men painted in France in the early part of the twentieth century. Their paintings influenced many other artists of their time.

Henri Matisse was born in a small town in France in 1869. He grew up in a wealthy family and showed no early interest in art. Then, while recovering from surgery in 1890, he began to pass the time by painting. From then on, he considered himself a painter.

In his paintings, Matisse used color in a way that no artist had before. His bold and unusual use of color let the viewer see the world in a new way. When he grew ill and could no longer paint, Matisse did not give up being an artist. He cut out large and colorful paper shapes and arranged them on a canvas. In this way, he was able to create beautiful art until the end of his life.

Marc Chagall was born in a small Russian town in 1887. His family was poor, but young Chagall begged his parents to let him study art. After working for some time as an artist, Chagall decided to go to Paris. He studied and worked there for four years before returning to Russia, where he met and married his wife. Eventually, he moved his family to Paris, where he stayed for most of his remaining years. His later work included murals and stained-glass windows.

Chagall's paintings remind some people of scenes they might see in a dream. Animals and people float in the air. Wonderfully unusual colors add to the dream-like quality. Chagall used ideas from Russian fairy tales and Jewish folktales in many of his works.

Matisse and Chagall each used art and color to show ideas in new and unusual ways. Today their paintings hang in fine museums all over the world. Along with artists like Monet and Picasso, they are considered pioneers of modern art.

1. How were Matisse and Chagall alike?

   ○ **A.** Both painted dream-like scenes all their lives.
   ○ **B.** Both lived in Russia and moved to Paris.
   ○ **C.** Both came from poor families.
   ○ **D.** Both painted in France in the early twentieth century.

2. How are Chagall's paintings like those of Matisse?

   ○ **F.** They include fairy tale scenes.
   ○ **G.** They use color in unusual ways.
   ○ **H.** They are all portraits.
   ○ **J.** They are made of cut-out shapes.

3. What did young Matisse and young Chagall have in common?

   ○ **A.** Both had wealthy families.
   ○ **B.** Both grew up in small towns.
   ○ **C.** Both had an early interest in art.
   ○ **D.** Both grew up in France.

4. How did Chagall and Matisse differ toward the end of their lives?

   ○ **F.** Matisse worked in France, while Chagall worked in Russia.
   ○ **G.** Matisse painted fairy tale scenes, while Chagall painted only portraits.
   ○ **H.** Matisse made cut-outs, while Chagall created murals.
   ○ **J.** Matisse used only black and white, while Chagall used bolder colors.

5. According to the writer, what do Matisse and Chagall have in common with Monet and Picasso?

   ○ **A.** They were all pioneers of modern art.
   ○ **B.** They all painted until the end of their lives.
   ○ **C.** They all stopped painting to do other types of art.
   ○ **D.** They all discovered a love for art early in their lives.

Name _____

Information and Study Skills

Read each question. Fill in the circle next to the best answer.

1. If you wanted to write a report about Thomas Jefferson, where might be a good place to start?
    - ○ **A.** a web site about United States presidents
    - ○ **B.** the encyclopedia
    - ○ **C.** newspaper articles
    - ○ **D.** primary source documents

2. Which two words or phrases might you use to begin your search for information about Thomas Jefferson?
    - ○ **F.** president; Thomas
    - ○ **G.** politician; U.S. president
    - ○ **H.** Jefferson; U.S. president
    - ○ **J.** history; Jefferson

3. Where might you find the most information about Monticello, Jefferson's home?
    - ○ **A.** a web site about Monticello
    - ○ **B.** the White House
    - ○ **C.** a trade book about historical buildings
    - ○ **D.** an almanac

4. What might recent magazine or newspaper articles contribute to your report?

- ○ **F.** historical information about Jefferson
- ○ **G.** a summary of the important facts of Jefferson's career
- ○ **H.** a personal account of Jefferson's daily life
- ○ **J.** new information that has been found about Jefferson

5. What is an example of a primary source?

- ○ **A.** a book about United States presidents
- ○ **B.** Jefferson's published letters
- ○ **C.** an article in a history magazine
- ○ **D.** an encyclopedia entry

Name _____

Word Parts *ven* and *graph*

Read each sentence. Then find the meaning of the underlined word. Fill in the circle next to the best answer.

1. Before there were telephones or e-mail, some people relied on <u>telegraphs</u>.
   - ○ **A.** railroad tracks
   - ○ **B.** early forms of computers
   - ○ **C.** devices for sending messages
   - ○ **D.** mail carriers

2. With the <u>advent</u> of long-distance telephones, people used telegraphs less and less.
   - ○ **F.** coming or arrival
   - ○ **G.** catalog selling
   - ○ **H.** advertising
   - ○ **J.** addition

3. The teacher <u>intervened</u> as the two students began to argue.
   - ○ **A.** interviewed
   - ○ **B.** came between
   - ○ **C.** participated
   - ○ **D.** entered

4. The <u>biography</u> of Elizabeth I provided much information about England.
   - ○ **F.** theater production
   - ○ **G.** television show
   - ○ **H.** personal journal
   - ○ **J.** written history

5. The group will <u>convene</u> today to decide which student should be in charge.
   - ○ **A.** move out
   - ○ **B.** send away
   - ○ **C.** look around
   - ○ **D.** come together

STOP

F

Name _____

Plurals

Read each sentence. Then find the singular form of the under-lined word. Fill in the circle next to the best answer.

1. A flock of <u>sheep</u> grazed peacefully in the meadow.
   - ○ **A.** sheep
   - ○ **B.** sheeps
   - ○ **C.** sheepes
   - ○ **D.** sheepe

2. Ted bought two <u>loaves</u> of bread from the bakery.
   - ○ **F.** loafs
   - ○ **G.** loave
   - ○ **H.** loaf
   - ○ **J.** loav

3. My favorite <u>stories</u> come from a book of Irish myths.
   - ○ **A.** storie
   - ○ **B.** storys
   - ○ **C.** store
   - ○ **D.** story

4. We rented a couple of <u>videos</u> about sharks yesterday.
   - ○ **F.** videoe
   - ○ **G.** video
   - ○ **H.** videos
   - ○ **J.** vidoe

5. The tree <u>branches</u> swung wildly in the wind.
   - ○ **A.** branc
   - ○ **B.** branchs
   - ○ **C.** branch
   - ○ **D.** branche

G Name _____

Suffixes *-ent/-ence, -ant/-ance, -able/-ible, -ate*

Read each sentence. Then find the meaning of the underlined word. Fill in the circle next to the best answer.

1. Myra gave an <u>excellent</u> speech at the assembly.
   - ○ **A.** relating to an ability to excel
   - ○ **B.** without excelling
   - ○ **C.** having the quality of excelling
   - ○ **D.** in the direction of excelling

2. Everyone spent an <u>enjoyable</u> afternoon at the park.
   - ○ **F.** the ability to enjoy
   - ○ **G.** providing enjoyment
   - ○ **H.** without enjoyment
   - ○ **J.** the state of enjoying

3. I have a <u>preference</u> for the color blue.
   - ○ **A.** in a way that prefers
   - ○ **B.** capable of preferring
   - ○ **C.** without preferring
   - ○ **D.** the act of preferring

4. The ants at the picnic were a real <u>annoyance</u>.
   - ○ **F.** in a way that annoys
   - ○ **G.** capable of annoying
   - ○ **H.** something that annoys
   - ○ **J.** the ability to annoy

5. My brother was <u>desperate</u> to find his lost homework.
   - ○ **A.** feeling despair
   - ○ **B.** able to despair
   - ○ **C.** lacking despair
   - ○ **D.** relating to despair

Name _____

Spelling

Find the correctly spelled word to complete each sentence.
Fill in the circle beside your answer.

1. It is important for people to have an _____ way of life.
   - ○ **A.** activve
   - ○ **B.** acteve
   - ○ **C.** activ
   - ○ **D.** active

2. One way to do this is to _____ regularly.
   - ○ **F.** exercis
   - ○ **G.** exercize
   - ○ **H.** exerciz
   - ○ **J.** exercise

3. A regular run or walk can make a big _____ in how a person feels.
   - ○ **A.** difference
   - ○ **B.** differance
   - ○ **C.** differense
   - ○ **D.** differents

4. Mark says he feels _____ after his morning run.
   - ○ **F.** fantastik
   - ○ **G.** fantastick
   - ○ **H.** fantastic
   - ○ **J.** fantastice

5. He carries two orange _____ with him for quick energy.
   - ○ **A.** halfs
   - ○ **B.** halfes
   - ○ **C.** halvs
   - ○ **D.** halves

6. Anna is _____ about other kinds of activities.

- ○ **F.** curius
- ○ **G.** curious
- ○ **H.** curiuos
- ○ **J.** curiuse

7. She has visited several workout _____.

- ○ **A.** studios
- ○ **B.** studioes
- ○ **C.** studioze
- ○ **D.** studiose

8. Anna understands the _____ of keeping fit.

- ○ **F.** importense
- ○ **G.** importence
- ○ **H.** importance
- ○ **J.** importanse

9. She knows it takes _____ to stick with a regular workout routine.

- ○ **A.** courege
- ○ **B.** courije
- ○ **C.** courige
- ○ **D.** courage

10. The benefits are more energy and a _____ improvement in strength.

- ○ **F.** noticeable
- ○ **G.** noticible
- ○ **H.** noticeible
- ○ **J.** noticable

Name _____

Vocabulary

Read the sentences. Then find the word that means the opposite of each underlined word. Fill in the circle next to the best answer.

1. All of the girls on the camping trip were <u>friends</u> from school.
   - ○ **A.** classmates
   - ○ **B.** enemies
   - ○ **C.** students
   - ○ **D.** buddies

2. The campground <u>prohibited</u> loud music.
   - ○ **F.** listened
   - ○ **G.** forbade
   - ○ **H.** allowed
   - ○ **J.** encouraged

3. Everyone unpacked their bags <u>rapidly</u>.
   - ○ **A.** neatly
   - ○ **B.** slowly
   - ○ **C.** quickly
   - ○ **D.** carefully

4. Rebecca became <u>distressed</u> after she tripped over a rock.
   - ○ **F.** calm
   - ○ **G.** anxious
   - ○ **H.** clumsy
   - ○ **J.** worried

5. Her sprained ankle was beginning to <u>swell</u>.
   - ○ **A.** hurt
   - ○ **B.** heal
   - ○ **C.** expand
   - ○ **D.** shrink

Go on ⇨

Read the dictionary entry. Then look at each sentence and find the meaning of the underlined word. Fill in the circle next to the best answer.

> **store** (stôr) *n.* **1.** A place where goods are sold; a shop. **2.** A stock or supply reserved for future use. **3.** A great quantity. — *tr. v.* **stored, stor•ing, stores. 1.** To put away for future use.

6. The family kept a <u>store</u> of canned food in the basement for emergencies.
   - ○ **F.** a supply reserved for future use
   - ○ **G.** a shop
   - ○ **H.** a large shelf
   - ○ **J.** to put away for future use

7. She reminded the others to <u>store</u> their food safely.
   - ○ **A.** a place to buy things
   - ○ **B.** a supply for future use
   - ○ **C.** to put in storage
   - ○ **D.** to regard highly

8. Michael was excited to go to the new sporting goods <u>store</u> in town.
   - ○ **F.** a great quantity
   - ○ **G.** to put in storage
   - ○ **H.** a sports park
   - ○ **J.** a place where goods are sold

Read the dictionary entry. Then read each question and fill in the circle next to the best answer.

> **lib•er•ty** (lĭb′ ər tē) *n., pl.* **lib•er•ties** The right to act, believe, and express oneself as one chooses. [Latin, *lĭber*, free.]

9. From which word did *liberty* originally come?
   - ○ **A.** liberties
   - ○ **B.** library
   - ○ **C.** liber
   - ○ **D.** right

10. Which word has the same origin as *liberty*?
    - ○ **F.** license
    - ○ **G.** liberal
    - ○ **H.** freedom
    - ○ **J.** limit

STOP

Name _____

Grammar

Complete each sentence with the correct pronoun or pronouns.
Fill in the circle next to the best answer.

1. Tresha and _____ began to practice the long jump.
   ○ **A.** I
   ○ **B.** my
   ○ **C.** me
   ○ **D.** mine

2. _____ will compete at the track meet this weekend.
   ○ **F.** She and I
   ○ **G.** She and me
   ○ **H.** Her and me
   ○ **J.** Her and I

3. Coach Rivas took _____ aside and gave us some good pointers.
   ○ **A.** she and I
   ○ **B.** she and me
   ○ **C.** her and me
   ○ **D.** her and I

4. We think this could be _____ best chance to win.
   ○ **F.** ours
   ○ **G.** we
   ○ **H.** us
   ○ **J.** our

5. _____ do the coaches plan to enter in the relay race?
   ○ **A.** Who
   ○ **B.** Whom
   ○ **C.** Whose
   ○ **D.** Who's

6. _____ bag was left on the bus?

     ○ **F.** Who   ○ **H.** Whose

     ○ **G.** Whom   ○ **J.** Who's

7. Tresha said it was _____.

     ○ **A.** hers   ○ **C.** her

     ○ **B.** its   ○ **D.** my

Read each sentence. Fill in the circle next to the best answer.

8. Correct the double negative in the following sentence by changing the underlined part.

I have not never won a gold medal before.

     ○ **F.** I have not won no gold medal before.

     ○ **G.** I have never won a gold medal before.

     ○ **H.** I have won a gold medal before.

     ○ **J.** I haven't never won a gold medal before.

9. Choose the word or words that correctly replace the underlined part of the following sentence.

They're not going to give out ribbons this year.

     ○ **A.** They are

     ○ **B.** Their

     ○ **C.** They will

     ○ **D.** They were

10. Choose the word or words that correctly replace the underlined part of the following sentence.

It is never too late to begin practicing.

     ○ **F.** Its'

     ○ **G.** Its

     ○ **H.** It's

     ○ **J.** It was

(STOP)

Name _____

Writing Skills

Read each numbered sentence or pair of sentences. Then find the sentence or sentences that use nouns and pronouns most clearly. Fill in the circle next to the best answer.

1. When Tom and Jill saw the painting, Tom and Jill wanted to buy it.

    ○ **A.** When they saw the painting, they wanted to buy it.
    ○ **B.** When Tom and Jill saw the painting, we wanted to buy it.
    ○ **C.** When they saw the painting, Tom and he wanted to buy it.
    ○ **D.** When Tom and Jill saw the painting, they wanted to buy it.

2. We bought two cups from a potter and his wife. They are big and blue.

    ○ **F.** We bought two cups from a potter and his wife. The cups are big and blue.
    ○ **G.** We bought two cups from them. They are big and blue.
    ○ **H.** We bought them from them. The cups are big and blue.
    ○ **J.** We bought them from a potter and his wife. They are big and blue.

3. Mr. Milam introduced the artist. He is from Puerto Rico.

    ○ **A.** He introduced the artist. He is from Puerto Rico.
    ○ **B.** Mr. Milam introduced the artist. The artist is from Puerto Rico.
    ○ **C.** Mr. Milam introduced him. He is from Puerto Rico.
    ○ **D.** He introduced him. Mr. Milam is from Puerto Rico.

4. Molly and her mom went to the exhibit. She bought tickets for her.

   ○ **F.** They went to the exhibit. Molly bought tickets for her mom.
   ○ **G.** They went to the exhibit. She bought tickets for her.
   ○ **H.** Molly and her mom went to the exhibit. Molly bought tickets for her mom.
   ○ **J.** She and her mom went to the exhibit. She bought tickets for her.

5. The museum director gave him a tour. The mayor enjoyed the afternoon.

   ○ **A.** He gave the mayor a tour. He enjoyed the afternoon.
   ○ **B.** The museum director gave the mayor a tour. The mayor enjoyed the afternoon.
   ○ **C.** The museum director gave him a tour. He enjoyed the afternoon.
   ○ **D.** He gave him a tour. The mayor enjoyed the afternoon.

New Frontiers: Oceans and Space

Level 6, Theme 6

Theme Skills Test Record

Student _____ Date _____

Student Record Form	Possible Score	Criterion Score	Student Score
Part A: Cause and Effect	5	4	
Part B: Following Directions	5	4	
Part C: Categorize and Classify	5	4	
Part D: Drawing Conclusions	5	4	
Part E: Information and Study Skills	5	4	
Part F: Prefixes *de-, dis-, ex-, inter-, per-, pre-, pro-*	5	4	
Part G: Prefixes *ad-, ob-*	5	4	
Part H: Words with *ie* or *ei*	5	4	
Part I: Word Parts	5	4	
Part J: Spelling	10	8	
Part K: Vocabulary	10	8	
Part L: Grammar	10	8	
Part M: Writing Skills	5	4	
TOTAL	80	64	
		Total Student Score x 1.25 =	%

Name _____

Cause and Effect

Read the passage and answer the questions that follow.
Fill in the circle next to the best answer.

Waves of Destruction

Tsunamis are very large ocean waves. They are caused by earthquakes or volcanoes on the sea floor. These waves can be larger and more destructive than waves caused by hurricanes. Tsunamis can be harmful to people and structures that are in their path. They can strip a beach of sand and destroy trees and other plants.

Tsunamis travel quickly across the ocean. While they are moving quickly, they are not very high. As they get into shallow water near shore, they slow down. As the wave slows, it grows in height. Tsunamis can reach the shore with heights of thirty, sixty, or even ninety feet.

On March 28, 1964, there was an earthquake off the coast of Alaska. This earthquake triggered tsunamis going both east and west across the Pacific Ocean. The fast-moving waves reached cities separated by thousands of miles of ocean.

One tsunami hit the Alaskan coast. The town of Whittier, Alaska, suffered ten million dollars in damage to property. Thirteen of the seventy people who lived there were killed. Crescent City, California, was hit by a tsunami just over four hours after the earthquake. One of the tsunamis also struck the coast of Hilo, Hawaii.

The earthquake off the Alaskan coast also caused many landslides. The flow of rock and soil into the water caused smaller, local tsunamis. No system was in place for detecting landslides, so people had no warning of the oncoming waves. In response to this event, the Alaska Tsunami Warning Center was formed. Now there is a way to warn people of any local tsunami threat.

Go on

1. What causes a tsunami?
   - ○ **A.** hurricanes
   - ○ **B.** earthquakes or volcanoes
   - ○ **C.** fast-moving water
   - ○ **D.** destruction of beaches

2. What causes a tsunami to grow in height?
   - ○ **F.** moving steadily over deep water
   - ○ **G.** speeding up in shallow water
   - ○ **H.** slowing down in shallow water
   - ○ **J.** speeding up in deep water

3. What caused the Alaskan landslides in 1964?
   - ○ **A.** a tsunami
   - ○ **B.** an earthquake
   - ○ **C.** a hurricane
   - ○ **D.** a rainstorm

4. What happened when rock and soil from the landslides hit the ocean?
   - ○ **F.** They caused local tsunamis.
   - ○ **G.** They caused another earthquake.
   - ○ **H.** More landslides were set off.
   - ○ **J.** They protected the coast from tsunamis.

5. What is one **positive** effect of the 1964 Alaskan tsunamis?
   - ○ **A.** The small town of Whittier, Alaska, got new buildings.
   - ○ **B.** Cities separated by thousands of miles had something in common.
   - ○ **C.** People everywhere learned something about Alaska.
   - ○ **D.** The Alaska Tsunami Warning Center was formed.

Following Directions

Read the flyer for **Space Flight Camp**, and answer the questions that follow. Fill in the circle next to the best answer.

Space Flight Camp This Summer

Are you interested in learning about space exploration? Have you ever dreamed of becoming an astronaut? Make those dreams come true! Space Flight Camp provides the perfect opportunity to learn more about the space program. You'll even get the chance to train in some of the very same facilities that NASA astronauts use. Come join Space Flight Camp!

First, you'll need to decide when to attend Space Flight Camp. The following two-week summer sessions still have spaces available:
Session 1: June 12–June 26
Session 2: July 6–July 20
Session 3: August 1–August 15

To enroll in Space Flight Camp, you must request an application from our headquarters in Florida. Please send a typewritten request to Space Flight Camp, 1010 Facility Road, Orlando, Florida 12545. An application will be mailed to you in five to seven days.

Along with your completed application, provide
☉ a permission letter from your parents or guardian,
☉ a letter of recommendation from someone in your community,
☉ a $20 refundable deposit.

While you are waiting for your application to arrive in the mail, you can prepare for camp. Here are some things to do:
☉ First, schedule an appointment with a doctor for your camp physical exam.
☉ Next, go to the library and read about the space program. Find what interests you. List things you want to do or learn at Space Flight Camp. Bring this list with you.
☉ Finally, go shopping. Keep in mind that you will need comfortable shorts and T-shirts, sneakers, swimsuit, soap, shampoo, toothpaste, and toothbrush. We will provide sheets, towels, and space suits for practice.

Go on ➡

1. To join Space Flight Camp, what is the first thing you must decide?
   - ○ **A.** when to make a doctor's appointment
   - ○ **B.** what clothes to pack
   - ○ **C.** how to get to camp
   - ○ **D.** which session to attend

2. How can you request an application?
   - ○ **F.** by calling the headquarters in Florida
   - ○ **G.** by filling out the form on the flyer
   - ○ **H.** by sending a typewritten note to the headquarters
   - ○ **J.** by going to the library

3. Which three things should be included with the application?
   - ○ **A.** a list of things to do at camp, a $20 deposit, and sneakers
   - ○ **B.** a permission letter, a letter of recommendation, and a $20 deposit
   - ○ **C.** a permission letter, a typewritten request, and a library book
   - ○ **D.** shampoo, toothpaste, and a space suit for practice

4. To prepare for camp, what should you do first?
   - ○ **F.** Make an appointment for a physical exam.
   - ○ **G.** Go to the library to read about the space program.
   - ○ **H.** Make a list of things you want to learn and do at camp.
   - ○ **J.** Begin to pack your bags.

5. Which of the following should you pack for camp?
   - ○ **A.** a space suit for practice
   - ○ **B.** sneakers
   - ○ **C.** sheets
   - ○ **D.** towels

Name _____

Categorize and Classify

Read the passage and answer the questions that follow. Fill in
the circle next to the best answer.

Mysterious Manatees

Men sailing with Christopher Columbus in 1493 reported seeing
mermaids sitting on top of rocks in the ocean. Later, sailors told stories
of seeing the humps of giant sea serpents in the water. Actually, what the
sailors saw were probably manatees.

Manatees are large, torpedo-shaped mammals that live in warm seas,
bays, and rivers in several parts of the world. Manatees are related to the
dugongs, and both are classified as sea cows, or Sirenians. Another species
of sea cow, the *Hydrodamalis stelleri*, became extinct long ago.

Manatees have small front flippers and flattened tails that propel them
through the water. They are gentle creatures that graze mainly on sea
grasses. Like whales and walruses, manatees must come to the water's
surface every fifteen or twenty minutes to breathe.

In the United States, the Florida manatee lives along the coasts of the
Gulf of Mexico and the Atlantic Ocean from Louisiana to Virginia during
the summer. In winter these manatees live in the warm waters off the
coast of Florida. They grow up to fifteen feet long and can weigh as much
as two thousand pounds. When left alone, they live to be about thirty
years old.

Manatees were once almost extinct. Large numbers of manatees
swimming near boats were killed every year. They collided with the boats
or became tangled in fishing lines or nets and drowned. Some were shot
by thoughtless people.

In the late 1970s, the Manatee Sanctuary Act was passed in Florida.
This act protects the animals in their winter habitats. Boats are no longer
allowed in manatee areas. Although manatees are still in danger of extinc-
tion, their chances for survival have improved greatly.

1. Ancient sailors thought the creatures they saw belonged to what category?
   - ○ **A.** large fish, like sharks and swordfish
   - ○ **B.** mammals, like whales and dolphins
   - ○ **C.** mythical beings, like sea serpents and mermaids
   - ○ **D.** inanimate objects, like rocks and shells

2. In which category do manatees actually belong?
   - ○ **F.** dugongs
   - ○ **G.** sea cows
   - ○ **H.** *Hydrodamalis stelleri*
   - ○ **J.** large fish

3. How are manatees like whales and walruses?
   - ○ **A.** They must come to the surface to breathe.
   - ○ **B.** They are the world's largest animals.
   - ○ **C.** They graze on sea grasses.
   - ○ **D.** They live around the southeastern United States.

4. Why is the Florida manatee classified by that name?
   - ○ **F.** It was first discovered by sailors near Florida.
   - ○ **G.** It lives year round in waters off the coast of Florida.
   - ○ **H.** It makes its winter home off the Florida coast.
   - ○ **J.** The name distinguishes it from the Louisiana manatee.

5. In which of these ways can the Florida manatee be classified?
   - ○ **A.** as one of the state's symbols
   - ○ **B.** as a threat to swimmers and boaters
   - ○ **C.** as an overproducing species of animal
   - ○ **D.** as an endangered species

Name _____

Drawing Conclusions

Read the passage and answer the questions that follow. Fill in the circle next to the best answer.

A Deep-Sea Discovery

In 1977, a team of scientists made a remarkable discovery. They were exploring an area 8,000 feet under the sea. Their instruments had recorded unusual activity and temperature changes in the area. That made the scientists think they might find geysers or hot springs there. When they reached the bottom, they did find hot water pouring out of vents in the ocean floor. But they also found a surprise — a community of strange creatures that could survive without the sun!

Living near the vents were giant clams one foot wide. There were bright red tube worms up to twelve feet long. Scientists found blind white crabs and shrimp with no eyes crawling through the total darkness of the deep. Many of the animals were new species that had never been seen before.

Scientists were puzzled. Without the sun, how could plankton make food? Without plankton, how could an ocean food chain start? The team that explored the hot water vents did not include any biologists or experts on ocean life. They collected water from the site and took it back for biologists to study.

The biologists found an unusual kind of bacteria in the water samples. The bacteria lived on minerals in the hot water and used the heat of the earth for energy. These special bacteria were the key to solving the mystery. They were the first link in the food chain. They made life possible for all the larger creatures in the vent community.

Since the 1977 discovery, scientists have found similar hot vents in other parts of the ocean. There may be many new creatures yet to be discovered in these strange communities at the bottom of the ocean.

Go on →

1. What information tells you that scientists were not expecting to discover living things near the deep ocean vents?
   - ○ **A.** They had recorded temperature changes in the area.
   - ○ **B.** They were exploring special bacteria.
   - ○ **C.** They were looking for geysers and hot springs.
   - ○ **D.** There were no biologists or ocean life experts on the team.

2. What evidence helps you conclude that the deep-sea animals need something that comes from the vents?
   - ○ **F.** Some of the animals cannot see.
   - ○ **G.** The water coming from the vent is hot.
   - ○ **H.** The animals are found only near the vents.
   - ○ **J.** Some of the animals were species that had never been seen before.

3. What can you conclude from the questions that puzzled the scientists?
   - ○ **A.** The scientists did not know much about plankton.
   - ○ **B.** The scientists had not been on the ocean floor before.
   - ○ **C.** Most ocean food chains start with plankton.
   - ○ **D.** Most ocean food chains start with bacteria.

4. What can you conclude from the description of the shrimp and crabs that lived near the vents?
   - ○ **F.** Minerals in the water cause blindness.
   - ○ **G.** Vision is not that important for survival on the dark ocean floor.
   - ○ **H.** Deep-sea animals have excellent vision.
   - ○ **J.** All deep-sea animals are blind.

5. Which is a conclusion scientists might make based on the 1977 discovery?
   - ○ **A.** There could be life near deep-sea vents in other parts of the ocean.
   - ○ **B.** There are probably cold water vents in other parts of the ocean.
   - ○ **C.** Minerals in the water from vents may poison ocean animals.
   - ○ **D.** There is no life near deep-sea vents in other parts of the ocean.

Name _____

Information and Study Skills

Study the registration form. Then answer the questions that follow. Fill in the circle next to the best answer.

Marine Life Aquarium and Study Center
Visitor's Registration

Name: _____
          last   first   middle

Street Address: _____

City: _____ State: _____ ZIP: _____

Home Phone Number (including area code): _____

1. Have you visited the aquarium before? ❏ Yes ❏ No
2. Would you like to volunteer at the aquarium? ❏ Yes ❏ No
3. Would you like to receive our monthly newsletter? ❏ Yes ❏ No
4. Please write comments, questions, and suggestions in the space below:

_____

---

1. Which of the following information is asked for on the application?
    ○ **A.** middle name
    ○ **B.** work phone number
    ○ **C.** age
    ○ **D.** date

2. How could you use the form to find out more about one of the fish at the aquarium?
    ○ **F.** Put a question mark by your phone number.
    ○ **G.** Write a question in the space below item number 4.
    ○ **H.** Check "No" as your answer to the first question.
    ○ **J.** Write your school address at the bottom of the form.

Study the information on the time line. Then read each question and fill in the circle next to the best answer.

Events in the Career of Jacques Cousteau

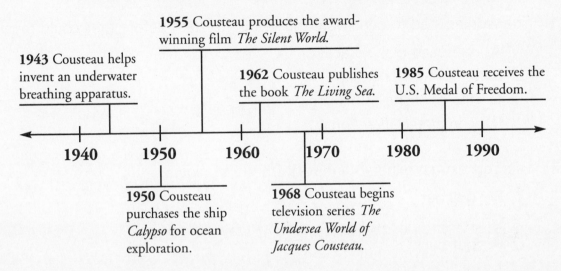

1955 Cousteau produces the award-winning film *The Silent World.*

1943 Cousteau helps invent an underwater breathing apparatus.

1962 Cousteau publishes the book *The Living Sea.*

1985 Cousteau receives the U.S. Medal of Freedom.

1940   1950   1960   1970   1980   1990

1950 Cousteau purchases the ship *Calypso* for ocean exploration.

1968 Cousteau begins television series *The Undersea World of Jacques Cousteau.*

3. According to the time line, what event occurred in 1943?
   - A. Cousteau helped invent an underwater breathing apparatus.
   - B. Cousteau produced a film.
   - C. Cousteau published a book.
   - D. Cousteau received the Medal of Freedom.

4. In what year did Cousteau begin a television series?
   - F. 1950
   - G. 1955
   - H. 1962
   - J. 1968

5. Which event occurred **before** Cousteau produced *The Silent World*?
   - A. Cousteau received the Medal of Freedom.
   - B. Cousteau began a television series.
   - C. Cousteau purchased the *Calypso*.
   - D. Cousteau published *The Living Sea*.

Name _____

Prefixes *de-, dis-, ex-, inter-, per-, pre-, pro-*

Read each sentence. Then find the meaning of the underlined word. Fill in the circle next to the best answer.

1. The workers had to <u>deactivate</u> the security system before they could repair it.
   - ○ **A.** between making active
   - ○ **B.** before making active
   - ○ **C.** the opposite of making active
   - ○ **D.** completely in action

2. Laborers <u>extract</u> minerals and rock from the mine.
   - ○ **F.** pull out
   - ○ **G.** repair
   - ○ **H.** put back
   - ○ **J.** pull through

3. We had to stop at a checkpoint at the <u>international</u> border.
   - ○ **A.** the opposite of national
   - ○ **B.** out of the nation
   - ○ **C.** completely national
   - ○ **D.** between nations

4. The student's <u>perception</u> of the painting was different from the teacher's.
   - ○ **F.** knowledge gained between the senses
   - ○ **G.** knowledge gained through the senses
   - ○ **H.** knowledge gained before the senses
   - ○ **J.** the opposite of gaining knowledge

5. The scientist found bones from a <u>prehistoric</u> animal.
   - ○ **A.** through a certain period of time
   - ○ **B.** between two periods of time
   - ○ **C.** a time after things were written down in history
   - ○ **D.** a time before things were written down in history

STOP

G Name _____

Prefixes *ad-* and *ob-*

Read each sentence. Then find the meaning of the underlined word. Fill in the circle next to the best answer.

1. I ran out of <u>adhesive</u> tape when I was wrapping the package.
   - ○ **A.** having a sticky quality
   - ○ **B.** lacking the ability to stick
   - ○ **C.** before being able to stick
   - ○ **D.** against the quality of sticking

2. The chess player <u>advanced</u> to the next level in the competition.
   - ○ **F.** moved through
   - ○ **G.** the opposite of moving
   - ○ **H.** moved forward
   - ○ **J.** moved with

3. The students did not <u>object</u> to the lengthy assignment.
   - ○ **A.** the opposite of argue
   - ○ **B.** being able to argue
   - ○ **C.** argue together
   - ○ **D.** argue against

4. The speaker will <u>advocate</u> recycling glass and cans from the school cafeteria.
   - ○ **F.** speak in favor of
   - ○ **G.** be able to speak
   - ○ **H.** speak against
   - ○ **J.** the opposite of speak

5. The athlete's <u>objective</u> was to perform her very best.
   - ○ **A.** the opposite of setting a goal
   - ○ **B.** something one works toward
   - ○ **C.** working through something
   - ○ **D.** getting between one thing and another

STOP

Name _____

Words with *ie* or *ei*

Read each sentence. Find the sentence in which the underlined word has the long *a* sound, as in *aim*. Fill in the circle next to the best answer.

1. ○ **A.** Can you <u>believe</u> the size of that fish?
   ○ **B.** A horse pulled the <u>sleigh</u> through the snow.
   ○ **C.** I felt a sense of <u>relief</u> when I found my lost wallet.
   ○ **D.** The <u>ceiling</u> fan cooled the room nicely.

2. ○ **F.** Did you know a beluga whale can <u>weigh</u> a ton?
   ○ **G.** There was a <u>brief</u> meeting before the tour began.
   ○ **H.** If you try hard, you can <u>achieve</u> great things.
   ○ **J.** The astronaut <u>received</u> flowers for her birthday.

3. ○ **A.** The <u>chief</u> benefit of exercise is good health.
   ○ **B.** <u>Neither</u> of us can go this weekend.
   ○ **C.** We need a large <u>piece</u> of cloth to cover the tank.
   ○ **D.** How much <u>freight</u> can the shuttle carry?

Read each sentence. Find the sentence in which the underlined word has the long *e* sound, as in *key*. Fill in the circle next to the best answer.

4. ○ **F.** My <u>friend</u> Matt is a marine scientist.
   ○ **G.** How long did Queen Elizabeth <u>reign</u>?
   ○ **H.** <u>Seize</u> that dog before he gets out again!
   ○ **J.** That tiny kitten is always getting into <u>mischief</u>.

5. ○ **A.** The rainstorm brought <u>relief</u> from the drought.
   ○ **B.** The bride's <u>veil</u> was sheer and beautiful.
   ○ **C.** There is a nice park in our <u>neighborhood</u>.
   ○ **D.** The team decided to <u>forfeit</u> the game.

Name _____

Word Parts

Read each sentence. Then find the meaning of the underlined word. Fill in the circle next to the best answer.

1. The secretary's job was to <u>transcribe</u> the notes from the meeting.
    - ○ **A.** make a recording of
    - ○ **B.** listen to and remember
    - ○ **C.** be an important part of
    - ○ **D.** put spoken words into writing

2. The girls took a <u>portable</u> radio with them to the beach.
    - ○ **F.** able to be seen
    - ○ **G.** able to be carried
    - ○ **H.** used at a distance
    - ○ **J.** reasonable in price

3. Computers and e-mail are changing the <u>telecommunications</u> industry.
    - ○ **A.** a system of televising communication
    - ○ **B.** the technology of communicating at a distance
    - ○ **C.** a special form of written communications
    - ○ **D.** the technology of reproducing sounds

4. The statue was placed in the park to <u>commemorate</u> the first moon exploration.
    - ○ **F.** honor the memory of
    - ○ **G.** allow people to write about
    - ○ **H.** send images across a distance
    - ○ **J.** provide a reason for visiting

5. The medicine helped to <u>minimize</u> the jellyfish sting.
    - ○ **A.** see at a distance
    - ○ **B.** be mindful of
    - ○ **C.** make smaller
    - ○ **D.** carry help to

Name _____

Spelling

Find the correctly spelled word to complete each sentence.
Fill in the circle beside your answer.

1. Juana wanted to _____ the earth from an orbiting spacecraft.
   - ○ **A.** ubserve
   - ○ **B.** obsurve
   - ○ **C.** observe
   - ○ **D.** ubsurve

2. She had to _____ her parents to let her make the trip.
   - ○ **F.** pursuade
   - ○ **G.** persuede
   - ○ **H.** presuade
   - ○ **J.** persuade

3. They finally made the _____ to let her go.
   - ○ **A.** decision
   - ○ **B.** deecision
   - ○ **C.** dicision
   - ○ **D.** ducision

4. Juana went through a _____ but tough training program.
   - ○ **F.** breif
   - ○ **G.** breef
   - ○ **H.** brief
   - ○ **J.** breaf

5. The _____ of her knowledge was increased a great deal.
   - ○ **A.** eckstent
   - ○ **B.** extent
   - ○ **C.** exstent
   - ○ **D.** ekstent

Go on ⟹

6. She even learned to _____ the crew in some of their tasks.
   - ○ **F.** asist
   - ○ **G.** asisst
   - ○ **H.** assistt
   - ○ **J.** assist

7. Before liftoff, Juana had an _____ with the press.
   - ○ **A.** interview
   - ○ **B.** enterview
   - ○ **C.** innterview
   - ○ **D.** innerview

8. Then she sat back and waited to see the _____ sights from space.
   - ○ **F.** unbeleivable
   - ○ **G.** unbelievable
   - ○ **H.** unbelieveable
   - ○ **J.** unbeleiveable

9. Juana enjoyed floating to the shuttle's _____ due to the lack of gravity.
   - ○ **A.** ceeling
   - ○ **B.** cieling
   - ○ **C.** ceilling
   - ○ **D.** ceiling

10. Juana was happy to return to Earth, _____ of how much fun she had had in space.
   - ○ **F.** reguardless
   - ○ **G.** regardless
   - ○ **H.** regardeless
   - ○ **J.** reegardless

Name _____

Vocabulary

Choose the word that best completes each sentence. Fill in the circle next to your answer.

1. <u>Pilot</u> is to <u>airplane</u> as <u>astronaut</u> is to _____.
- ○ **A.** space
- ○ **B.** spacecraft
- ○ **C.** flying
- ○ **D.** moon

2. <u>Famous</u> is to <u>unknown</u> as <u>considerate</u> is to _____.
- ○ **F.** generous
- ○ **G.** prominent
- ○ **H.** thoughtful
- ○ **J.** cruel

3. <u>Surprise</u> is to <u>astonish</u> as <u>fortify</u> is to _____.
- ○ **A.** please
- ○ **B.** strengthen
- ○ **C.** shock
- ○ **D.** weaken

Read each sentence. Then find the meaning of each underlined word. Fill in the circle next to the best answer.

4. The first lunar-landing <u>mission</u> was a great scientific achievement.
- ○ **F.** an activity that people like to do
- ○ **G.** a flight where people miss their target
- ○ **H.** a special job on which people are sent
- ○ **J.** an uncompleted project

5. The <u>astronomer</u> adjusted the large telescope using a computer.
- ○ **A.** a person who studies the stars
- ○ **B.** someone who writes science fiction books
- ○ **C.** a specially trained astronaut
- ○ **D.** someone who is good with machines

Read each question. Then fill in the circle next to the best answer.

6. Which dictionary entry word would you look under to find the meaning of the idiom *on the right track?*
   ○ **F.** on
   ○ **G.** the
   ○ **H.** right
   ○ **J.** track

7. Which dictionary entry word would you look under to find a run-on entry for *notably?*
   ○ **A.** notation
   ○ **B.** note
   ○ **C.** notable
   ○ **D.** notary

8. Which dictionary entry word would you look under to find the meaning of the idiom *get a kick out of* ?
   ○ **F.** kick
   ○ **G.** get
   ○ **H.** out
   ○ **J.** of

Read each dictionary entry. Then answer the questions. Fill in the circle next to the best answer.

> **cat • a • log** or **cat • a • logue** (kăt′l ôg′ *or* kăt′l ŏg′)*n.* A list of items with a description of each item: *a library card catalog.*
>
> **nei • ther** (nē′ thər *or* nī′ thər) *adj.* Not either; not one nor the other: *Neither shoe fits comfortably.*

9. What is another way to correctly spell *catalog?*
   ○ **A.** catalogs
   ○ **B.** catlog
   ○ **C.** catalogue
   ○ **D.** cataloge

10. In what way are the two pronunciations of *neither* different?
    ○ **F.** in the way the first syllable is pronounced
    ○ **G.** in the way the syllables are stressed
    ○ **H.** in the way the second syllable is pronounced
    ○ **J.** in the way it is spelled

Grammar

Read each question. Fill in the circle next to the best answer.

1. Which choice shows the prepositional phrase in the following sentence?

    When the winds began blowing, the sailboat was tossed violently in the sea.

    ○ **A.** When the winds   ○ **C.** was tossed
    ○ **B.** began blowing   ○ **D.** in the sea

2. Which choice shows the prepositional phrase in the following sentence?

    While the lightning flashed, the captain steered the ship toward the shore.

    ○ **F.** toward the shore   ○ **H.** captain steered
    ○ **G.** steered the ship   ○ **J.** While the lightning flashed

3. Which of the following sentences contains a prepositional phrase used as an adverb?

    ○ **A.** The rough waves poured over the ship's deck.
    ○ **B.** The water on the deck threatened the sailors' safety.
    ○ **C.** Many sailors on the ship were frightened.
    ○ **D.** The captain of the ship was hopeful that they would reach the shore safely.

4. Which of the following sentences contains a prepositional phrase used as an adjective?

    ○ **F.** As the storm grew worse, the ship started taking on more water.
    ○ **G.** The sailors began putting on their life vests.
    ○ **H.** "Will we survive this storm?" wondered the captain of the ship.
    ○ **J.** Luckily the storm started to die down as the ship neared the shore.

5. Which of the following sentences is punctuated correctly?

    ○ **A.** Ouch! The stove is hotter than I thought it would be!
    ○ **B.** Ouch the stove is hotter, than I thought it would be!
    ○ **C.** Ouch the stove is hotter than I thought it would be!
    ○ **D.** Ouch the stove, is hotter than I thought it would be!

6. Which of the following sentences uses abbreviations correctly?

   ○ **F.** The dr. Brown who lives at 111 Oak blvd is the man I am seeking.

   ○ **G.** The Dr. Brown who lives at 111 Oak blvd. is the man I am seeking.

   ○ **H.** The Dr Brown who lives at 111 Oak Blvd is the man I am seeking.

   ○ **J.** The Dr. Brown who lives at 111 Oak Blvd. is the man I am seeking.

7. Which of the following sentences uses commas correctly?

   ○ **A.** I am more interested in Mercury, Mars and Jupiter than in Pluto.

   ○ **B.** I am more interested in Mercury, Mars, and Jupiter than in Pluto.

   ○ **C.** I am more interested in Mercury, Mars and, Jupiter than in Pluto.

   ○ **D.** I am more interested in Mercury Mars, and, Jupiter than in Pluto.

8. Which of the following sentences uses commas correctly?

   ○ **F.** The new student in our class La Shawn Lewis, plans to go to Space Camp this summer.

   ○ **G.** The new student in our class, La Shawn Lewis plans to go to Space Camp this summer.

   ○ **H.** The new student in our class, LaShawn Lewis, plans to go to Space Camp this summer.

   ○ **J.** The new student in our class LaShawn, Lewis plans to go to Space Camp this summer.

9. In which sentence is the dialogue punctuated correctly?

   ○ **A.** "That sounds like fun," said Jan. "I would like to go, too!"

   ○ **B.** "That sounds like fun". said Jan. "I would like to go, too!"

   ○ **C.** "That sounds like fun," said Jan "I would like to go, too!"

   ○ **D.** "That sounds like fun" said Jan. "I would like to go, too!"

10. In which sentence is the book title capitalized correctly?

   ○ **F.** Have you read the book entitled *Mars is a Planet of Many Extremes*?

   ○ **G.** Have you read the book entitled *Mars Is A Planet Of Many Extremes*?

   ○ **H.** Have you read the book entitled *Mars Is a Planet of Many Extremes*?

   ○ **J.** Have you read the book entitled *Mars Is a Planet of many Extremes*?

Name _____

Writing Skills

Read each pair of sentences. Then choose the best way to combine them into a sentence with prepositional phrases. Fill in the circle next to the best answer.

1. It was warm at the beach. It was sunny at the beach.
   - ○ **A.** Warm, it was sunny at the beach.
   - ○ **B.** At the beach, warm and sunny it was.
   - ○ **C.** It was warm and sunny at the beach.
   - ○ **D.** It was warm at the beach, and it was sunny.

2. Dad ran quickly toward the lifeguard chair. The lifeguard chair was on the shore.
   - ○ **F.** Dad ran quickly and the lifeguard chair was on the shore.
   - ○ **G.** Toward the lifeguard chair on the shore, Dad ran quickly.
   - ○ **H.** Dad ran, toward the lifeguard chair, and the lifeguard chair was on the shore.
   - ○ **J.** Dad ran quickly toward the lifeguard chair on the shore.

Read each pair of sentences. Then choose the best way to combine them into a sentence using commas. Fill in the circle next to the best answer.

3. Mom likes to gather shells at the beach. Kit has no interest in shells.
   - ○ **A.** Mom likes to gather shells at the beach but Kit, has no interest in shells.
   - ○ **B.** Mom likes to gather shells at the beach, but Kit has no interest in shells.
   - ○ **C.** Mom likes to gather shells, at the beach but Kit has no interest in shells.
   - ○ **D.** Mom likes to gather shells at the beach but Kit has no interest, in shells.

4. Dad likes to fish in the surf. Kit prefers to ride the waves on his surfboard.

○ **F.** Although Dad likes to fish in the surf, Kit prefers to ride the waves on his surfboard.

○ **G.** Although, Dad likes to fish in the surf Kit prefers to ride the waves on his surfboard.

○ **H.** Although Dad likes to fish, in the surf Kit prefers to ride the waves on his surfboard.

○ **J.** Although Dad likes to fish in the surf Kit, prefers to ride the waves on his surfboard.

5. It is finally time to leave. Everyone wants to stay a little longer.

○ **A.** When it is finally, time to leave everyone wants to stay a little longer.

○ **B.** When it is finally time to leave, everyone wants to stay a little longer.

○ **C.** When, it is finally time to leave everyone wants to stay a little longer.

○ **D.** When it is finally time to leave everyone, wants to stay a little longer.